MARY

Mother of God,
Mother of the Poor

THEOLOGY AND LIBERATION SERIES

Ivone Gebara
and
Maria Clara Bingemer

MARY

Mother of God,
Mother of the Poor

Translated from the Portuguese by
Phillip Berryman

ORBIS BOOKS

Maryknoll, New York 10545

BT
613
.G4213
1989

First published in the United States of America by Orbis Books, Maryknoll, NY 10545, and in Great Britain by Burns & Oates, Wellwood, North Farm Rd., Tunbridge Wells, Kent TN2 3DR

Published originally by Editora Vozes Ltda., Petrópolis, R.J., Brazil, under the title *Maria, Mãe de Deus e Mãe dos Pobres*

Original edition © 1987 by CESEP—São Paulo
English translation © 1989 by Orbis Books
All rights reserved
Manufactured in the United States of America

Bible translations are from the NAB, with adaptations where necessary to reflect the authors' Portuguese texts.

ORBIS/ISBN 0-88344-638-3
           0-88344-637-5 (pbk)

Theology and Liberation Series

In the years since its emergence in Latin America, liberation theology has challenged the church to a renewal of faith lived in solidarity with the poor and oppressed. The effects of this theology have spread throughout the world, inspiring in many Christians a deeper life of faith and commitment, but for others arousing fears and concerns.

Its proponents have insisted that liberation theology is not a subtopic of theology but really a new way of doing theology. The Theology and Liberation Series is an effort to test that claim by addressing the full spectrum of Christian faith from the perspective of the poor.

Thus, volumes in the Series are devoted to such topics as God, Christ, the church, revelation, Mary, the sacraments, and so forth. But the Series will also explore topics seldom addressed by traditional theology, though vital to Christian life — aspects of politics, culture, the role of women, the status of ethnic minorities. All these are examined in the light of faith lived in a context of oppression and liberation.

The work of over one hundred theologians, pastoral agents, and social scientists from Latin America, and supported by some one hundred and forty bishops, the Theology and Liberation Series is the most ambitious and creative theological project in the history of the Americas.

Addressed to the universal church, these volumes will be essential reading for all those interested in the challenge of faith in the modern world. They will be especially welcomed by all who are committed to the cause of the poor, by those seeking to establish a more solid link between faith and politics, prayer and action.

Publisher's Note

We have made it a practice in this series to replace the conventional authorial "we" with "I." The authors of this book, however, have not only written the whole of it together, but made the point that this joint approach is a particular characteristic of the way women "do" theology in Latin America — that they would rather work in "solidarity" than alone. The "we" therefore means "both of us" throughout, and has deliberately been retained.

Contents

vii

Abbreviations and Short Forms

BCCs   Christian base communities

DS   Denzinger-Schönmetzer. *Enchiridion Symbolorum, definitionum et declarationum de rebus fidei et morum.* Translations of DS in the current work are from Josef Neuner and Heinrich Roos, *The Teaching of the Catholic Church* (TCC), ed. Karl Rahner (New York: Alba House, 1967)

LG   *Lumen Gentium.* Vatican II, Dogmatic Constitution on the Church

Puebla   Final Document of Third General Conference of Latin American Bishops, held at Puebla, Mexico, in 1979. Translations are from *Puebla and Beyond* (Maryknoll, N.Y.: Orbis Books, 1979)

MC   *Marialis Cultus.* Paul VI, Encyclical Letter

MD   *Munificentissimus Deus.* Pius XII, Apostolic Constitution defining the Assumption

REB   *Revista Eclesiástica Brasileira*

RM   *Redemptoris Mater.* John Paul II, Encyclical Letter

TCC   See above, under DS

Introduction

Hail Mary of the people,
Hail Mary of God,
Mary of the oppressed,
set your children free. . . .

Voices ring out heartily, with energy, singing about the press-
ing need for the liberation of the poor in countryside and city.
And the voices sing of Mary, ally of the oppressed, faithful to
the struggle of the poor. All timbres of voice are mixed. Out of
this polyphony we single out the voices of the women, whose
alliance with Mary is becoming important at this moment in
Latin America — this moment when women, along with all the
oppressed in our continent, are stirring to win their rights.

It has been these voices in particular that have led us to conceive of a Marian theology whose starting point is women and
Latin America. Our guiding principle has been a critical concern to
grasp what underlies the different official and popular Mariologies.
We have brought to the surface the anthropological characteristics
that guide Mariologies; we have proposed an anthropological
foundation that is unifying, realist, and pluri-dimensional; and,
moreover, we have emphasized the existential plight of the people,
which is latent or manifest in Marian devotions.

Some new hermeneutical perspectives, whose purpose is to
provide a Marian theology built upon the basis of the people's
actual experience, have enabled us better to grasp God's revelation in woman. We have intentionally tried to indicate to what
extent our own personal circumstances and social position as
writers have a bearing on our hermeneutical effort.

Our biblical reflection treads along the path of that same
anthropology and hermeneutics. It begins with a reflection on
the idea of the Kingdom of God, with a reading based on the
Jesus movement, the prophetic tradition that preceded the Jesus

movement, and the tradition of women who actively took part in establishing the justice of the Kingdom. Out of their midst and out of the midst of the people arises the figure of Mary, who is heir to the hopes of the poor and at the same time gives a new impulse to those hopes. Our re-readings of the New Testament texts about Mary are an effort to involve our creative imagination and retrieve both what has been said and what has not been said, so we may be able to understand Mary, woman-and-people, in the power of her battle on behalf of *life.*

Out of fascination with Mary people have sought to pin down certain aspects of her life, aspects connected to the life of the people of God, and this is what has constituted Marian dogma. We have carried out a new reading of that dogma, starting from the poor and from the spirit of our own age so that we might be able to re-focus our eyes on the depictions of Mary which are "old," yet new and beautiful.

What faith confesses of Mary in doctrine is expressed experientially in devotion to Mary in Latin America. We have tried to take up some aspects in the history of Marian devotion, and then, on the basis of a reflection on the deep meaning of apparitions, cures, and miracles, we have sought to understand some aspects of the phenomenon of Guadalupe, the paradigm of Latin American devotion to Mary.

The people have creatively made the Magnificat their own; the song of the Virgin of Nazareth has become their song, especially in the experience of Christian base communities, where the people strive to be a small sign of the Kingdom in the midst of the outrageous injustices on our continent.

Mary's song is the people's song:

> The day will come when
> raising their gaze
> all will see freedom
> reign on this earth.
>
> My soul magnifies the liberating God,
> My spirit rejoices in God my Savior,
> For God has remembered the oppressed people,
> and has made God's servant the mother of the
>   forgotten. . . .

CHAPTER I

Toward a New Anthropological Perspective

The Mariologies written till now have generally not bothered to make clear and explicit the anthropological[1] conceptions governing their procedure. They have left this work to the assumptions of their readers or, more likely, assumed that the anthropological question in Mariology is firmly settled.

The kind of anthropology which has generally been most evident in theological work and particularly in Mariology has been Platonic in origin, although this has never been made explicit systematically. As we know, this anthropology is based on a dualistic principle that divides reality into a world of things accessible to the senses and the True World or the World of Ideas. This division also touches all aspects of human reality, from the way we know, to our work, to love, to relationships between persons, to gender divisions.

Little thought has been given to how much this anthropological vision entails a deep separation between men and women, that is, how in this division men are regarded as the thinking beings par excellence, the ones closest to the ideals of perfection, while women are seen as second-class beings, with little affinity for the things of the spirit or for thinking; hence in this view women are remote from true ideas and from divinity. It is only through men that they can have access to the divine.

In all honesty, we cannot ignore the fact that it was part of the cultural ethos of the ancient Jewish people, with their rigid patriarchal traditions, to regard women as subordinate. This was not a dualistic anthropology along Platonic lines, but was an aspect of a hierarchical society, where men and women never stood on an equal plane.

Traditional Mariology speaks of Mary in "feminine" terms, idealizing her on the basis of certain qualities said to be feminine, a determination which is made from a male viewpoint. Thus Mary is "retrieved" by this traditional anthropologico-theological vision and goes on to justify it insofar as she is a product of that vision. So Mary, mother of Jesus, mother of God, as presented by the androcentric and patriarchal world, far from provoking conflicts, actually strengthens the cultural foundations of that world to the extent that she also becomes its great Mother. So we can understand the problems the leading figures of the patriarchal religious system have with re-readings of the life of Mary. These will entail a re-reading of the foundations of the patriarchal system, since we are touching on the very nature of maternity.

We believe the task of theology is not only to explain faith in God, but to explain it intelligibly at each point in history and appropriately for different cultural contexts. One element in this intelligibility is a new development in anthropology that can do justice to the complexity of the human reality.

When we speak of developing anthropology we especially have in mind emphasizing some fundamental lines governing our understanding of what human beings are and what their task in history is. This is not the place for us to speak of various anthropologies coming one after another or simultaneously existing in different places and moments of human history. Our anthropological perspective is theological: and more precisely our intention is to do the groundwork for a Marian theology. Therefore when we speak of anthropology we are speaking of theology. The horizon of Christian faith is always present; it dwells within us; it helps us to lay out an egalitarian anthropology.

It is from this viewpoint that we will attempt to sketch in

broad outline the characteristics of the anthropology guiding our view of Marian theology, delineating the central point at which one anthropological vision gives way to another. In this sense, we can say that we are moving:

— from a male-centered to a human-centered anthropology;

— from a dualistic to a unifying anthropology;

— from an idealist to a realist anthropology;

— from a one-dimensional to a pluri-dimensional anthropology.

1. FROM A MALE-CENTERED TO A HUMAN-CENTERED ANTHROPOLOGY

The vision of Christian theological literature is typically centered on "man" (male-centrism), on "man" as male gender.[2] "Man" is the main actor in salvation history. That perspective projects on to God the cultural traits of the male gender in all realms of existence. The human-centered vision posits humankind, man and woman, as the center of history. This vision has innumerable consequences, especially in theology. It is humankind, man-and-woman, who builds history, and who is interrelated one to another and with divinity. The male human is not the only mediator, but simply *a* mediator in the relationship between God and humankind. The content of the words "mediator" and "mediation" must be clarified in this anthropological sketch. This is not mediation in the sense of a middle term, an intermediary between one being and another, or even of a mediator as a subject who would establish some kind of connection between beings. Such language expresses a hierarchical framework which seems alien to the New Testament experience and to the stance we are taking. From the perspective of the incarnation, God totally takes on human flesh; this is evident in statements such as, "one who sees me, sees the Father," "one who claims to love God and hates a brother or sister, is a liar," "I was hungry and you fed me," "I was naked and you clothed me." We are God's presence to one another; we are God's call to conversion for one another. Hence all humankind is temple, God's dwelling. Relationship with God takes place through the mysterious relationship between persons, in whom God's own

Spirit dwells. The hierarchical framework of mediations, still strongly present in Judaism and other ancient religions, is thus overcome. In committing their lives to the emergence of the Kingdom, all become a "priestly race," that is, all humankind becomes bearer of divinity and capable of revealing it.

The human-centered perspective is set within this new light. The male expression of humanity is not privileged at the expense of the female; nor is there any effort to affirm the latter in order to downgrade the former. A human-centered anthropology seeks to grasp the revelation of the divine all throughout the human and accepts the historical and theological consequences of this stance. The first great consequence will be the relativization of male-centered cultural patterns. Theology has been written on the basis of such patterns, and they have penetrated deeply into the values of both the Eastern and Western worlds, distorting the way human life is experienced and aggravating the subjection of women to men, a subjection supposedly based on divine right. Traditional anthropology has concealed the part played by women in great historical events, or it has reduced that activity, subordinating it to the activity of men, even though on different occasions some women have broken these age-old chains and have become paradigms of a new social order. For the moment we shall not focus on the exceptions, although their importance is irrefutable, but rather on what is regarded as the normal way men and women relate. An anthropology with human-centered characteristics is the only kind that will enable us to work out a Marian theology that can recover the historic activity of women for the sake of the Kingdom and which consequently can do justice to Mary, women, men, and ultimately to humankind created in the image and likeness of God.

At this point in our reflection, a question could be posed: How is God's transcendence made manifest in this new perspective? Might we not be introducing something that changes the presence of that transcendence that is particularly present in men? No question about it: that is our aim and we accept the consequences. The time has come to criticize the general nature of egalitarian expressions within theology which nevertheless do not fit the actual experience of women and men. The aim of such criticism is to restore the value of each human being through what is autonomous and original in each one. This is related to God's presence, to the presence of transcendence in man and in woman.

Transcendence is not synonymous with higher experience or other-worldly experience, or experience beyond history, or to put it another way, transcendence is not a break in the forward course of history. God's transcendence is manifest in God's creature. It is we, in our relativity within history, in our limits and frailty, who grasp the existence of transcendence, who speak about it, who express it. This all happens because it is within us, in our capacity as human beings to go beyond ourselves, even though we do not always exercise that capacity and do not always allow it to flourish in the ongoing events of history.

We believe that the human-centered perspective is actually revelatory of divine and human transcendence because it does not diminish the human by dividing it into higher and lower beings, but rather does justice to God's absolute justice, which is above our hypotheses and theories about God.

2. FROM A DUALISTIC TO A UNIFYING ANTHROPOLOGY

Opposition between spirit and matter, common to Greek thought, has been a centuries-long legacy in the development of Christian theology. Its imprint is still visible today, and even when we think we have been freed from dualism, we are still somehow caught up in its snares, which are often subtle and tenuous. Hence we cannot claim that an absolute shift toward a unifying anthropology has taken place. The ancient split between spirit and matter still runs in our culture's blood and through our own veins, even when we try to claim something else.

On the one hand, unifying anthropology strives to overcome this dualism by affirming the deep unity of the human being, who is both material and spiritual, inseparably material and spiritual, so much so that we cannot conceive of the human being except on the basis of this reality which is proper to humans. When we say material and spiritual, we have to affirm this reality within the limits of the material nature of history. We grasp our spiritual make-up within the limits of our materiality. There is no love without a concrete loving expression; there is no seeking of the divine except on the basis of this history that we build and that builds us.

On the other hand, unifying anthropology seeks to affirm the existence of a single human history. It does not set two histories against each other as though there were a divine and a human history: rather it takes as its starting point this single history, scene of the conflicts, of the joys and sorrows of generations and generations of different peoples. This means that our true history is neither ahead of nor behind us, but is this history being built with sweat, blood, tears, in the unceasing advance of generations one after another. From this viewpoint, to say that the Word of God became flesh is not to say that previously the Word was outside history and that at a particular moment it entered history. We always work with temporal and chronological frameworks which, if on the one hand they make it easier to understand many things, also limit understanding since they hinder us from acquiring a more open stance, one more in accordance with the dimension of mystery inherent in human existence. To say that the Word became flesh is also to say that "in the beginning was the Word," that is, that the Word has always been, but that at a particular time we recognized it in the countenance of the man Jesus and in the countenance of humankind, so much so that we understand that true love for God is expressed in the practice of family-spirited love. From that point onward, there has been a qualitative shift in the history of humankind. This is the historic depth of the mystery of the incarnation, from which we must drink unceasingly with a thirst that can never be satisfied.

For a Marian theology the bases of a unifying anthropology not only restore the realism of human existence which shows the imprint of different periods of history, but they also bring human existence to share deeply in the mystery of the incarnation. The Word becomes flesh in human flesh, flesh of man and woman, historic flesh bearing the imprint of space and time, of life and death, of joy and sorrow, of building up and tearing down, ultimately of the conflict inherent in our being and in our history.

3. FROM AN IDEALIST TO A REALIST ANTHROPOLOGY

According to idealist anthropology, the truth of human beings is found not within history but in a world beyond history. History is but a transit, an interval, perhaps a "vale of tears," until true human life is made manifest. Such a stance has very serious consequences for ongoing history, for it leads to domination by minorities who believe the heavens have destined them for the role of guiding history, and correspondingly to a kind of conformity on the part of the masses who make up the majority, since they are convinced that it is hard to change paths already laid out.

While it is true that pain and suffering are part of the human condition, so are joy and the search for happiness—and that search begins here and now.

Idealism, like dualism to which it is closely linked, is always tempting to us. The world of our dreams and projections is always beautiful, harmonious, perfect. The real world in which we live, with its constant conflicts, its apparent or real contradictions, seems to weigh us down. Our desire changes the world; very often we live wrapped up in the world we desire or project, and we forget to look at reality in its beauty and ugliness, its cleanliness or filth. What most interests us is the "other world," the "other me," the "other reality." People discuss ideas, enter into endless controversies, but are incapable of seeing, of sensing, of detecting the challenge represented in the presence of the "man with the withered hand," or the "woman suffering a hemorrhage" in the middle of the crowd.

The problem with idealism is not simply that it holds that there is a "world of ideas" that are perfect and unchanging, but indeed there is also the problem that from the strictly anthropological viewpoint, idealism is a more or less veiled denial of human reality as it appears to us. Once human reality is denied or hidden, it can hardly be transformed. People tend to hide behind a certain number of values and virtues regarded as signs of perfection or even behavior patterns regarded as perfect in themselves. The fear of not fitting these pre-established virtues or behavior patterns prevents us from discerning personal and social reality with open eyes, with the eyes of those who want to see fearlessly so as to be capable of improving what exists, loving it and transforming or preserving it for the good of everyone.

Something similar happens with regard to Mary. From the idealist viewpoint, the only things perceived in Mary are her superhuman qualities, her virtues worthy of imitation, her capacity for unlimited affection and her limitless love. Such a being is overwhelming. The acceptable attitude toward her is one of unthinking submission. We say "unthinking submission" since many people do not allow themselves even the slightest critical thought so as to keep their ideal image of Mary intact. If anything touches this image, their whole world comes crashing down. Whether rich or poor, they equip themselves with all kinds of defense mechanisms in order to defend the figure of Mary, but at the same time they are defending their own securities, their myths, in an attempt to preserve what they have built up for themselves and perhaps for others. As we said previously, this is an image of the woman Mary that has been "retrieved" by a male-centered world, in an attempt to justify and preserve that world.

The idealist anthropological perspective prevents us from approaching the task of doing theology in another way, a theology starting from the ground of history, from the site of the incarnation of God's Word. It allows only a theology superimposed on reality, creating an unreal world in the attempt to make up for the crack opening in the human heart due to dissatisfaction, all kinds of dissatisfactions piling up one after another throughout history, and especially in the history of the wretched of the earth.

A realist anthropology, however, is not the same as pure objectivity. Indeed, there is no such thing. What exists is a mixture of objectivity and subjectivity; what exists is a plethora of interpretations, of hypotheses and theories about different facts. Facts do not exist without interpretation, which is their meaning. One cannot exist without the other. Thus realist anthropology does not deny subjectivity. At one level it affirms subjectivity as a fundamental component of reality, which is understood as that which encompasses us, affects us, constitutes us, and which enables us to arrive at a simple description of events, whether personal or social.[3]

At another level, realist anthropology observes and respects the laws that govern human life on its various levels and that govern the life of the stars, plants and animals, and indeed everything relating to human life in its various relationships with the entire universe. Hence there is no disrespect for the accomplishments of science, although those accomplishments may be viewed critically. All this is related to life, and life is basically related to God.

Realist anthropology provides Marian theology with a concrete support that can fit the changing reality of human existence. The "eternal," whether in values, persons, or deities, is always historical; that is, it always retains the imprint of time — it begins, grows, changes, ages, dies, is renewed. Such a perspective permits an ever new understanding of the figure of Mary. A model, a way of being, cannot be eternalized — rather the historic figure Mary must enter into dialogue with the time, the space, the culture, the problems, and the actual persons that relate to that figure. It is today's life that gives life to Mary's life in the past.

On the basis of these principles we can say that the "eternal truths" in Marian theology are first historic truths subject to the complexity, diversity, and change proper to human existence. This statement elevates all creation and does not exalt one period over another or one race over another. Thus we can see human history in a less rigid, less static, less dogmatic manner, without any pre-established models that could be presented as valid for all cultures, provided that a few tiny adaptations are made. This statement makes it possible for cultures to meet in their differences, to relate to one another, to make one another fruitful so as continually to encourage the outbreak of what is new, while protecting different aspects, and evolving in the continuous/discontinuous flow of history.

Theologically speaking, this assertion means accepting the creative power of the Spirit of God who is ever renewing all things, who effects rebirth, who restores energies, who brings back to life what seemed to be dead.[4]

4. FROM A ONE-DIMENSIONAL TO A PLURI-DIMENSIONAL ANTHROPOLOGY

What typifies one-dimensional anthropology is a kind of pre-determination of what human nature is; in other words, the starting point for its reflection is a closed definition of the human. It already knows what is human, natural, unnatural, true, false. One-dimensional anthropology works with clearly defined boundaries, and confronts us with alternatives: the human being is either this or that. The human being is first of all what it is defined to be, the ideal already set down; the human being is defined by those characteristics attributed to it, by differences laid down in relation to other beings, by those behavior patterns already judged to be proper to man or woman or not to be so.

The evolution of human beings throughout centuries of history is taken as something incidental. One-dimensional anthropology is really an expression of essentialist idealism from which arise all kinds of moral rigidity on all levels of human existence. Human beings and God are completely different and rather static. Therefore anything said that differs from what has already been said of God, and of men and women, is unacceptable. Only variations on what has already been said are acceptable. One-dimensional anthropology provides security, proposes a certain number of changeless certainties, and serves as the basis of all kinds of authoritarianisms. Those who accept it are closed to progress and to the great questions facing the world.

Seen theologically, one-dimensional anthropology conse-crates the male-centered vision as the one laid down and willed by God. Any contrary statement is regarded as denying the will of the Creator or as a refusal to accept that will. Hence, this anthropology cannot in any way ground efforts toward equality between men and women or even permit the working out of a Marian theology that might do justice to God and to humankind, God's image and likeness. What we mean to say is that one-dimensional anthropology consecrates male images of God and situates man, the male being, as the first and most important in the order of creation.

What typifies pluri-dimensional anthropology is that it takes into account the different dimensions of humankind as it has evolved through history and as countless elements have left their mark on it. The human being is not primarily a definition but rather a history within space and time. Within themselves human beings contain the animal, the vegetable, the mineral, the spiritual, the divine. They also contain good and evil, love and hatred, peace and violence, not as mutually exclusive but in a mixture that includes all these "ingredients." Thus human beings are not first good and then corrupted, nor first corrupted and then saved, but rather humans are this whole complex reality striving to explain themselves and to explain the world in an existence marked by internal division and marked by the nature of their being, which is conflictive and simultaneously limited and unlimited.[5]

Seen theologically, pluri-dimensional anthropology proposes a human-centered vision, reflecting profoundly on the complementary aspects of human reality — man and woman.[6] From this perspective of complementarity, it can then assess the radical tendencies that ignore the overall human reality and thus tend toward one or other extreme.

Marian theology finds in pluri-dimensional anthropology a divine-human foundation that enables it to view with justice and deep respect the "human phenomenon," which builds history and is created, loved, and saved by God.

Furthermore, a pluri-dimensional approach to anthropology enables us to develop a Marian theology in which the various aspects of relationship to Mary can take shape without one necessarily excluding the other. Each aspect is a sketch, an expression, a word about the human yearning for the divine that inhabits and constitutes the human being. Mary is the divine in the female expression of the human, the constitutive expression of what we call the integrally human.[7] Thus, the fierce abhorrence of what is different, manifested in the variety of persons and cultures, can give way to inexhaustible wonder at the dimensions discovered when we accept the mystery of our extraordinary diversity.

Enchanted by his own image, lost in his own beauty and certainty, Narcissus has to open up to the different avenues of life, to different dances, different beauties and certainties. Only in that way will he avert a death that results from being a prisoner of his own self-enchantment. Only in that way will he cease to "find ugly anything but the mirror," as the poet Caetano Veloso puts it in his work *Sampa*.[8]

5. FEMINIST ANTHROPOLOGY AND MARIAN THEOLOGY

If we are doing Marian theology as women who listen to the people of God and to ourselves, it seems that we must take on an important task, that of developing in broad outline an anthropology capable of going beyond the experience of "man" as normative for all human behavior. In our view, such an anthropology is not necessarily exclusive to women but it must be open enough to encompass the difference, multiplicity, non-homogeneity, and creativity of the human—man and woman.

We think the previous sections move in this direction and provide some anthropological elements, which insofar as they are deepened, can lead us along new paths. The aim of the present section is to shed further light on the much-debated issue of the specifically feminine in theology.

Today more than before, women are awakening to the reality of their own being and to the experience of an independent life. That is gradually making it possible for them no longer to be defined in terms of men, whether as complement or as subordinate. This experience is a qualitative step that in the future will lead to historic consequences not yet sufficiently appreciated.

There is an effort to find oneself, in both individual and group terms, to seek an understanding of one's "self" independently of predetermined definitions that limit one's being to a small sphere of influence. With some exceptions, women in the past have more or less accepted their situation as a kind of fate, and—starting with nursing babies and continuing through all phases of education—they have passed on to their sons and daughters this "programming" of a world divided into those who give orders and those who take them, into what is specific to men and what is specific to women. Not only that, they have even utilized the advantages such a situation offered them, accepting and cultivating an ambivalent situation. To their "lords," they seem fragile, dependent, and obedient, and yet it is they who are strong, who sustain the home, educate the children, and are often unappreciated victims who nevertheless endure everything for "love."

Today this situation is beginning to change in different places around the world. It is happening in its own way in Latin America, where women are taking on a different role, especially in the religious realm and indeed in doing theology. We need to make some preliminary observations in order to clarify the meaning of this new development.

In the Western world, as we know, man has always been identified with reason, and reason with spirit, and spirit with divinity. Hence men have always imagined themselves to be closer to divinity than women. Women's spiritual traditions have never met with much success, especially in Christian tradition. The power of patriarchy in different religious institutions has stifled them and relegated them to obscurity.[9]

As Maria Riley has said quite well,[10] rationality has always been the "province" of the male, while that of the female has been irrationality and intuition. For centuries, or more specifically till the advent of the European enlightenment and the subsequent scientific and social revolution emerging from it, this male rationality was seen predominantly in religion, and religion was therefore viewed as the great "civilizer" of the world. That situation underwent change insofar as rationality became increasingly identified with the scientific method, and the church for its part took a position of resistance to, and fear of, modernity. The church saw modernity as representing a threat to its power, which it claimed derived from a knowledge of the "sacred" that could accept no doubts or questioning.

Increasingly, the hierarchical structure of the church, the structure that holds the institution's power, took an ambivalent position: control was masculine and exercised by men, but the world of religion moved over to the feminine, that is, beyond the rationality of the world. That position also came to the fore in theological production. The clergy have continued to be those who produce theology without being very concerned about the progress being made in rationality by the world, except in a few cases, and then the "orthodoxy" of the various churches fought tenaciously against them. In the world of religion, things have to continue more or less the same. Changes are permitted to the extent they do not directly affect power over the sacred or the exercise of that power. Although this situation is not so typical of our own century, it still persists up to our own day and is felt with greater or lesser intensity throughout the whole bloc of Western Christian countries.

This is the context in which the "feminist revolution" is beginning to take place in theological circles. Previously submissive *consumers* of "small dosages" of theology sufficient for their own domestic use, women are now beginning to inquire about their faith and their relationship with God, and to do theology, thereby becoming *producers* of this type of knowlege.[11] In this respect their work is just beginning, still at the groundwork stage, still laying the foundation, often on slippery and shifting ground. However, this seems to be the moment when the anthropological question is posed most forcefully. Is there perhaps a female way, something proper to women, something specific in the way they do theology, that will distinguish them from men? Or, are we not at a privileged moment of creativity on the part of the woman/human that actually introduces a difference so great that it will lead us to speak of woman's own anthropology?

If the answer were related to what is specifically feminine in theology, we would be facing a serious anthropological issue that would oblige us to speak of male anthropology and female anthropology as two distinct, but intimately connected, realities. Such a pursuit, we believe, would not take us very far. It does not seem possible to discern peculiarly male characteristics, despite the biological differences that characterize man and woman.

The meaning of a feminine, or more precisely, a feminist anthropology, is closely connected to the historic moment in which we are living, the moment in which women's consciousness is breaking out into awareness of their age-old oppression and their age-old stance of compliance with and subjection to the oppressive structures of society and particularly of religion. In general, a feminist anthropology would be the expression of the awakening of the other half of humankind, the women's half, to living realities from which they have been alienated. If certain so-called feminine qualities are emphasized in this awakening, the aim is not to create an opposition between the qualities of men and those of women, since that would serve no purpose. From a dialectical viewpoint, the moment of affirming a thesis is always related to the moment of negating it for the sake of a new synthesis containing both elements. Hence what is important is the new synthesis that is going to emerge, even if the impression it gives is of opposition between two realities.

The evolution of science and of the various cultures proves every day how inappropriate it is to classify what might be proper to one or other gender, especially with regard to particular attributes.[12] Culture shapes our being and our being produces culture. Indeed, we are both product and producers of what we live, know, inherit, believe, and hope. Hence it is useless for us to try to define the "eternal" feminine or aspects of it. We will never find the "eternal" but only the provisional, the diverse, the manifold, which appears in different shades in the most varied cultural contexts and periods in history. If we emphasize one quality as essentially feminine in a particular culture, it will not be so in another culture, or even at different periods in the same culture.

In the light of these observations, can we even speak of a feminist theology at all? Only to the extent that women, as part of the human race, manage to express the living reality of their faith, a reality that has been stifled, kept dormant for centuries, and which must be restored for the sake of all humankind. From this viewpoint there is room for all efforts to recover women's contribution in early Christian tradition, to emphasize readings of the Bible in which women's participation is un-concealed, and to foster the search for women's participation in society and especially in the church throughout different ages in history and in different countries.

Our position is simply that, when women begin to acquire knowledge previously forbidden to them, efforts are made to define the specific way they do so, as though their being were essentially different from men's being. We think it is useless to search for this specific element; it can restrict the new and "revolutionary" event of women's theological awakening to the point where it is seen as simply their particular literary expression or the manifestation of the conditioning society imposes on them. This new development affects men's hold over the sacred as private property; it concerns the right to a form of expression not stamped in a male mold; it touches on the urgent need for power to be divided and shared in church institutions; indeed it affects all theology, insofar as theology must revise the way it addresses itself to men and women, who are both equally and historically dwelling places of God's Spirit.

It is in the light of this newness in our time, the newness of the Spirit of God in our history, that we lay out our thoughts in this book. What we say is in no way opposed to the numerous efforts toward a feminist expression of theology carried out by our colleagues in different countries around the world. We are merely attempting to situate these efforts in another light, pointing toward a synthesis that will encompass the rich diversity of the human.

Hence our exploration in Marian theology does not highlight the qualities of Mary/woman, qualities idealized and projected from different needs and cultures, but rather aims at a re-reading of Mary from the needs of our age, and especially from the insights provided by the awakening of women's historical consciousness.

6. ANTHROPOLOGY AND THEOLOGY: THE HUMAN WORD ABOUT GOD IN MARY

Discourse about God and the "things" of God is always a human discourse. Christian revelation is a human word about God, a word that becomes "divine word" for human beings. Therefore, it is within the limited reality of the human that one speaks the word about the divine.

The human word becomes divine word when it touches on the heart, the core, what is deepest in the human. This deepest aspect in turn points to the personal and collective history of human beings. It refers to that which in fact allows the right to life and respect for life for all beings. Hence, the various religious texts called "revelations" of the divinity point to something that affects the deep fulfillment of every human being. It is as though beyond the differences that distinguish us, we were walking on a common ground that impelled us to recognize that we are equal, similar, complementary to one another.

We can say, then, that everything comes from God or is God's initiative; and we can also say that it is always within the limit of the human that the experience of the divine is lived, pronounced, and communicated. This way of seeing the "things" of God has frequently not been taken into account or accepted. We seem to prefer the idealist perspective where God is regarded as an isolated being in God's own world, communicating with humankind which stands in the midst of the conflicts of history. Many people seem to find it reassuring to say that it was God in person who said such-and-such to so-and-so, but the question of how God might have spoken or written does not even come up. Little consideration is given to the human; little thought is given to the social and cultural conditions affecting one or other "word" said to be God's revelation or a word about God.

The contrary perspective, which we could call realist, attributes to the human all its density and worth, and perceives there the divine breaking through, in humankind's seeking and accomplishments in history. The human is not hidden beneath the divine, as though the divine were sometimes choking, sometimes caressing, sometimes heeding, and sometimes rejecting the human. The divine takes place in the human, in its entire flesh, in its precarious wholeness.

The kind of explanation whose starting point is the fact that discourse about God is a human discourse seems to allow enough openness for the "infinite" manifestations of the divine in the human. It seems to show greater respect for the complementary dimension of everything created and the presence of the divine in everything created.[13]

It is only from this angle that there can be a "human word" about Mary, a word that becomes "divine word" for human beings. Mary, a word filled with the human desire for fulfillment. Mary, word of hope, poetic word, word combining many longings.

Mary is more than "just Mary." She is more than the mother of Jesus; she is more than the people symbolized in a woman. Mary is divine creation of the human and in the human. Hence we can speak of God's "endless" revelation of God in Mary. Each period of history "reveals" or "projects" the desire for something sublime, extraordinary, small, great, but always full of hope in the figure of a woman, goddess, mother, wife. Mary, the Mother of Jesus, Mary of Nazareth, has entered into different human cultures, she has met their deities, has influenced them and been influenced by them. The face of Mary of Nazareth has become manifold, like human yearnings, like the responses of love. Those responses are both so different and yet similar. . . . They spring from what is hoped, and from the unexpected, from encounter and from failure to connect, in grace and its absence.[14] We are too small to understand its mystery and yet we are too great, for this wonder takes place in us. This is the refrain of human disproportion, whose melody the philosopher Pascal ever recalls to us in his *Pensées* on human greatness and insignificance.[15]

That is why we can speak of different Marian traditions, of different ways of reading Mary's countenance, and they do not have to be mutually exclusive. Mary has moved beyond the situation of individuals who have only one history. She has many stories which merge into history, linking the lives of individuals and multitudes.

The life of Mary of Nazareth is always taking place anew. Sometimes the main theme of the score stands out in a new way, because the arrangement and performance give it a harmony and a timbre as though it were something entirely new, a fresh composition and performance never heard before.

Hence when Mary's story is told we must be open to hearing new stories. She is part of the religious poetry of Christians and this cannot end, nor may it even be limited to a rigid dogmatics, which are incapable of accompanying the musical notes and creative rhythm of each age and each people. Mary is divine creation of the human. . . . And the divine and the human will be alive, as long as man and woman last.[16]

This extraordinary creative energy of human beings, this "soaring flight" despite the darkness of the times, is manifest in Mary, although in root form it is present in the experience of life and faith of a people. Mary somehow awakens this energy, draws it out, prompts it to overflow into different meaningful symbolic expressions, which go on to become part of the history of a people.

It is in the light of this anthropological perspective that we understand the various traditions of devotion to Mary and especially those related to Latin America, as we shall see in Chapter V. Before doing that, however, we must clarify the hermeneutical approach that guides our thinking.

CHAPTER II

Hermeneutics for a Marian Theology

1. THOSE WHO "LIVE IN GOD" AND THOSE WHO "LIVE IN HISTORY"—SOMETHING NEW IN HERMENEUTICS

In taking up hermeneutics, our aim is not to show how it has developed in theology or to lay out the nature of the different schools and theories, but rather to deal with an issue that we believe is basic for Marian theology and yet is hardly ever faced as a question relevant for any theological—and especially Marian—hermeneutics. This is the question of the faith relationship between believers within history and those who "live in God." Mary is one of the latter, and indeed she has a very important role among them.

Being connected to Mary is evidence of belief in life after death, that is, a belief that human life continues in God, no longer subject to the limitations of history. This belief, present in the earliest Christian tradition, was generally not part of the early stages of the history of the people of Israel, as narrated in the Old Testament, although one can say that the question of life after death is present in the book of Maccabees. Even given the absence of this belief in some stages of history, we can still say that all indications are that there is a connection between struggles during life—characterized by failure, political defeat, and early death—and the absolute human yearning to live, to see one's existence extended in a life of justice, all one's toils rewarded. It is a complex issue, but it is clear that the desire for eternal life has come to dwell in people's hearts and has become part of their belief. Moreover, faith in the resurrection of the flesh has been an integral part of the Christian creed from the beginning.

From this angle it is useful to recall that under various influences Christian tradition has individualized life after death so that each dead person remains "alive." Through their followers some of them carry on their activity in history, becoming involved in it, guiding certain events, entering into the conflicts of those still alive and taking sides with them. They do this because while alive they played outstanding roles or performed actions that were meaningful for the history of a group or a people.[1]

The new involvement in temporal and material history also reveals the limit on the activity of those who "live in God," a limit latently present in the conduct of those devoted to them. They, those who "live in God," cannot do everything since they are subject to the conditions and limits inherent in history itself. Taking note of this seems to reveal to some extent the limits of the human spirit and confirm our limited reality, no matter what our particular situation may be.

The individualization experienced on the level of personal and social relations with some of those who "live in God" does not contradict the traditional belief in the Church Triumphant as a body; that is, it does not contradict belief in the Church Triumphant as made up of all those who in victory after death "live in God," despite the "silence" of many of them in history. Not all those who "live in God" have adherents or are especially remembered.

On to those who "live in God" is projected the situation of those who "live in history," a limit-situation and yet one in which there is a yearning for the unlimited. Whatever in the life of those who "live in history" brings harmony, perfection, health, wholeness, safety, fulfillment, love—which are values of the yearning for the unlimited—is requested and sought from those who are "alive in God." Some of them, because of the virtues they practiced during their experience in history, have proven their human worthiness. These virtues seem to touch the deep human yearning for the unlimited, and this partly explains why some of those who "live in God" play a seemingly constant role in the history of humankind.

The yearning for the unlimited is a human characteristic and is expressed in the most varied manners. It is conditioned by class situation, culture, the values people embrace, the development of critical consciousness, the immediacy of events, the urgency of what is desired as a value and vital necessity. Although class situation is very important, certain ways in which the "yearning for the unlimited" is expressed seem to transcend it, establishing a supra-class situation around the "saint" or the one who "lives in God."[2] That no doubt entails great ambiguities and all kinds of contradictions. All we have to do is look at the way different groups associated with shrines act and how different interests come into play in devotion to those who "live in God."

The yearning for the unlimited can provide another focus for the question of devotion. This focus has less to do with admiration for the virtues of those who "live in God" and more to do with the desires of those in the act of admiration. For the act of admiration is interconnected with a multiplicity of desires that run through multitudes and individuals; as we have already noted, these desires take on different expressions in accordance with the needs of persons and of the moment. Many of these yearnings are linked to the surety that those who "live in God" are a kind of certain guarantee, an incontestable last resort within the insecure and fragile course of events, even if the yearning is not satisfied.

In conflicts in history and in day-to-day problems, trust between people is always being shaken, and always tends to be tenuous and fleeting. No one seems to think enough of the needs of others. The desires of the self prevail over the common good. By contrast, you can trust those who "live in God" and in particular you can express your problem and expect to be heard. Those living in God can meet human yearnings in a way that those living in history cannot, no matter what human qualities the former may have. Those living in God do not compete with the supplicant, but are simply bestowers of favors and so can pay attention to the problems of whoever comes pleading. Their main function in the unfolding of individual and group history is to aid supplicants, those who are still involved in day-to-day struggles, whether great or small.

Beyond Mary's special status in the history of Christian faith, she enters into the dynamic of human yearning with everything that the figure of woman evokes. Further on, we shall reflect on this specific aspect of Mary. At this point, we think it important to focus our reflection on the question of yearning and its implications in the religious relationship between the supplicant and the saint.

The desire of those living in history seems to continue in the desire of those living in God for history, thus indicating that the yearning for the unlimited has no limit. Besides, non-limit, non-satisfaction, non-fulfillment are inherent in human desire.[3]

How are we to understand the fact that yearning is unlimited? How are we to understand the fact that even those who "live in God" do not rest? Even they seem to be possessed by the same drive to desire things for history and in history. Underlying these countless questions, we can discern an anthropology that is deeply centered on history, on this history that is sequential, eventful, relative, limited, conflictive, as though the only "habitat" for human beings were this stage that players enter and exit for shorter or longer periods; players play larger or smaller roles, but all of them are ultimately actors and actresses in the same production. The place of human beings, whatever their condition, is this history. If they depart physically, their memory remains in the collective structure of history, which immortalizes them normally in a collective way, as one among successive generations. Subsequent generations immortalize only a few as individuals. Certain conditions are required for people to attain individual immortality in history, basically that during their lives they were striking expressions of the yearning for the unlimited and that they constituted at least provisional "responses" to that desire.

The relationship between those who "live in history" and those who "live in God" has many functions in human life, especially in the religious realm. Those who "live in God" embody our unlimited yearning for life, the expression of our attachment to this history, to this earth of which we have been woven. Could it be otherwise? We dare to say it could be, since the human possibilities for conceiving and living life are many and varied. Nevertheless, we operate within the bounds of Western culture which is marked by Christianity, and it is from that vantage point that we speak. In addition, we speak from Latin America, out of its history, influenced by different races and cultures, as well as from our own personal history. Hence it is always good to keep in mind that our interpretations or approaches to the human mystery are marked by a certain one-sidedness, stemming from our background.

The relationship between those who "live in history" and those who "live in God" also helps us break the profound feeling of abandonment and loneliness of human beings and especially of the poor and oppressed masses of all times and everywhere in the world. This feeling of abandonment can lead to inertia and fear. It is a feeling that paralyzes both an individual person and human masses. When the masses feel abandoned they tend to accept any hand stretched out to them that may provide a minimum of security, even if that hand goes on to enslave them.

Given this feeling of abandonment, human beings need a set of strong guarantees; they need a "rope" dropped down from heaven, one that can dispel their fear, relativize it, bring it down to levels that make it possible for them to act.

Religion, with the wide variety of divinities it embraces, also has the role of exorcising fear and quieting the feeling of abandonment. This does not mean that it provides easy answers for human beings, or that it is the "opium of the people," but rather that by directing people to their own deep reality it can ensure them on the symbolic level of the security they need to live. Hence, Mary is not just the prophetic woman or the liberating woman, or the mother par excellence; rather, Mary, and even Jesus, God, the saints, are "magic" words, which when they are pronounced are like a cry that springs from the heart and produces some relief from affliction. The cry for God and for those "living in God" is the cry for help, whatever that help may be. When a "holy name" is pronounced, something helpful takes place, just as deep breathing can remedy the lack of air and relieve asphyxia. This deep breathing can be individual or collective and can take on different forms.

To call on the name of Jesus or the name of Mary or of a saint to whom one is devoted is like a balm that is good for the whole body, for the life in each one of us. Hence, there is something about religion that eludes us, touches the mystery of the human being, something unutterable like a deep sigh, inexplicable like a loving gesture, mysterious like the act of surrendering one's life for the sake of many.[4]

We are expressing these thoughts in order to say that our analyses of Mary, made from a non-traditional viewpoint, do not destroy the mystery of her personal existence and the mystery of what she means for millions of believers. It is precisely because we want to safeguard this mystery that we are proposing something suggested by the spirit of our age and by our involvement in popular movements made up mainly of women. At each new historical moment for Christians, the mystery of Mary unveils a different facet, one that can deeply touch the needs of the poor and believing people. The countenance of Mary, symbol of the people, extends the theology of salvation, and places women in active participation on an equal basis with men, despite women's own independence. This perspective is not yet something achieved in our era, but it is being announced strongly and vigorously, and it brings life for the future.

Another and related aspect, which we regard as fundamental, is to perceive that the connection with those who "live in God" is part of what we call "spirituality," especially when seen from Latin American popular circles. Spirituality has to do with the way we feel "sustained" by the Spirit of God, by Mary, by Jesus, by the saints. . . . To speak of spirituality is to speak of "something" sustaining the materiality in which we live; it is to have a "feel" that the last word on life is not reduced to what our eyes see or to what our ears hear, or to what our activity can accomplish in history. To speak of spirituality is to speak of something more than the causality of things, than the connection of certain events, than what can be seen as inevitable, than the programs of parties and churches. To speak of spirituality is to take life back beyond pure facts, it is to bring in a "hope that can hope against every hope." To speak of spirituality is to run up against human limits and to live by breaking through those limits; it is to touch the limits of existence and "to ask for God's hand," to "grasp it," to feel that Mary is accompanying us "on the paths of life"; it is to walk those paths conversing with one's favorite saint. To speak of spirituality is to organize one's life around transcendence, whatever historic form it might take on in different cultural environments.[5]

In Latin America one can speak of a Marian spirituality in the sense described above. Mary is hope, mother, protector, she who does not abandon her children.

All that we have just said constitutes matter for hermeneutics, a matter for interpretation leading to a Marian theology that gives expression to our age. For a Marian theology it is not enough to analyze biblical texts and to analyze the texts of previous tradition. It is crucial to recognize what kind of human experience devotion to Mary, or relationship with her, is. In other words, we must ask to what kind of "yearnings," manifest or latent, our relationship with Mary, who "lives in God" and lives in us, belongs. Otherwise, we run the risk of overloading ourselves with artificial structures and superficially calling them "truths" of faith, without questioning their purpose, their reality, or their relation to us.

We see hermeneutics not simply as the study of an ancient text so as to bring it closer to us. Hermeneutics also has to do with us, with bringing human beings closer to themselves; it has to do with a frank and sincere discussion that we ought to have on the basis of our experience. This is the hermeneutics of experience that must be carried out with no fear of uncovering what is simply human, in its frailty and greatness, its limit and transcendence.

2. BIBLICAL HERMENEUTICS FOR REVEALING THE ROLE OF WOMEN

Within Christian communities it is commonly accepted that the New Testament texts came after the initial events, namely, the life and activity of Jesus and of Mary and the first disciples. Nevertheless, although on the level of reason this is seemingly accepted as true, it is often not accepted in many of our behavior patterns and even in the concrete practice of our faith.

We do not know how to relate to the text as what it really is:

an interpretation and a catechesis by and for the early church. The New Testament texts read the life of Jesus and the people around him as a re-reading of the Old Testament, under the influence of new events. Certain foundational events of Jewish faith in the Old Testament reappear in a new perspective in the New Testament. Thus we cannot read the New Testament as a text independent of the Old Testament, and we cannot read the events related in the New Testament as absolutely apart from everything experienced in early Jewish culture. Events like the movement of many Jews to Egypt during a period of famine, the story of Joseph, the son of Jacob, the suffering of the people under the domination of the Pharaoh, the exodus from the land of slavery, the prophetic message during the period of the kingdom in Israel, the messianic promises—all return in the New Testament with another coloring and in another context, reinterpreted on the basis of the great event of Jesus and his movement.

With these observations we want to emphasize how important it is both to read the text starting from the context in which it was produced and to read the text from within the reader's own situation and conditions today. In this sense, re-reading is indispensable and even inevitable. Nevertheless, we cannot ignore the problems of hermeneutics, that is, the interpretation of the text that starts from its context. The Western world has generally sought to understand the sacred texts through "scholarly methods" or "church authority" without being sufficiently aware of all the problems inherent in the texts of ancient cultures.[6]

We forever repeat a certain number of interpretations as though we were certain that events had happened precisely according to those interpretations and precisely as we have learned about them. The problem we are touching here is not one of theoreticians, but is observable in the activity of different persons or groups who regard the conflict of interpretations as an interpretative conflict within themselves. Hence we can say that the conflict of interpretations exists not simply outside us but rather within us, and it is conditioned by the period of history in which we live.[7]

As we say this, it becomes clear that it is our aim to create uncertainty over our "correct" interpretations, to generate insecurity and to show that despite everything, we scarcely know the "soul" of the texts. That soul eludes us; it belongs to another climate, to another cultural universe. Moreover, the text reveals some aspects of the period and its personages and conceals others.

The productions of religion are always cultural productions, as are interpretations. Hence when we interpret we are making such productions, and we must always ask ourselves what are the main keys in our reading and interpretation. Another element we regard as important is the fact that the sacred writer always writes for a particular community. Hence, it cannot be a matter of simplistically transferring what is said for one group to another, even though some things may be quite applicable.

If the productions of religion are always cultural productions, interpretations are in some way new religious productions, even though they make use of the same ancient matrix. In the ancient matrix each culture, each era, each ideological group seeks an interpretation and a challenge related to the demands of its stage of history. Thus, the "soul" of a text is continually renewed and recreated; it does not remain forever the same. It is like a musical score that receives new "soul" at each new playing, with each new arrangement made by different musicians. Unless it is played, the score remains a dead letter. It is the power of musicians, their talent, their circumstances, and the challenges of the era in which they and their audiences live that give new life to the musical text. In this regard it is important to remember that we know a good deal more about the age in which we live than we do of the long ago past and the past of ancient cultures whose roots are often so different and so distant from our own.

It is good also to remind ourselves that sometimes we fail to see the limits of the author or the authors of a biblical text. They certainly cannot tell us everything. They express a point of view and pass on some information, and as we have said, they pass over many other items of information. That being the case, we cannot take a fundamentalist attitude toward the biblical text as if everything written were the whole historic reality of an age and the whole truth about it.

The written text should always generate within us a suspicion, or better, questions about what has not been written, what has been lost or what has been omitted by choice. A written text is always selective. The author or authors choose some events they believe important, and they interpret them, while leaving aside others which from another perspective might be regarded as the most important. That being the case, the full history of the people of the Bible is much more than what has been written. For instance, St. John ends his Gospel by saying of Jesus, "There are still many other things that Jesus did, yet if they were written about in detail, I doubt there would be room enough in the entire world to hold the books to record them" (John 21:25).

The purpose of all we have been saying is related to the texts that speak about Mary. As we know there are very few of them in the New Testament tradition, but on the basis of these few texts and various traditions that have arisen in the midst of the people, each period in history seems to build an image of Mary and her activity in history both past and present. So we cannot say that the only truth about the life of Mary is in the little bit that the New Testament texts tell us. The fact that something is not written does not mean that it did not happen.

The announcing of the good news of the Kingdom, if it is actually good news for humankind, must of necessity involve the participation of men and women, even if the texts written by men and from a patriarchal viewpoint leave out the active participation of women, and in our specific case, that of Mary. That is the reason why we must take up a critical stance toward texts, interpretations, and data, a stance that can open space for us to reconstruct and recover the history of the past and thereby grasp the revelation of the God of life in the lives of women as well.

Besides these preliminary observations, which we regard as essential clarifications, there are today, as in the past, many aspects of a personal nature that leave their imprint on our interpretation of the texts and our stance toward theological reflection. We recall simply a few that we regard as especially important for this Mariological endeavor and which are connected with the lives of the authors of this essay. That is what the next section is about.

3. PERSONAL FACTORS CONDITIONING A HERMENEUTIC

We are both Latin American women striving to reflect on Mary and attempting an essay in Marian theology: women living on a continent marked by oppression, marked by the suffering and daily death of thousands of people, especially children, a continent marked by the scourge of hunger and by violence expressed in various ways; two women with different stories, who despite the privileges that come with being intellectuals feel and suffer with the oppressed women of the Third World and with them seek to say a word about liberation. The word we have to say, the word that engages us in this struggle, is a theological word. It is with profound humility and even with a certain trepidation that we dare to pronounce a theological word, especially because of the marvelous mystery enclosed in it. The theological word is not "scientific" in the ordinary sense of the term and is not subject to rigid laws. The theological word is a vital word, referring to the deep meaning of our activities, of our life and our death. It is connected to the life and death of whole peoples, of the great human masses, and in our case, to the great masses of Latin America, the overwhelming majority of whom are poor, enjoy no adequate quality of life, and lack respect, bread, love, and *justice.*

Our starting point for reading the reality in which we live and hence for reading sacred scripture, the Christian tradition and the theology produced in the Christian West, is a stance from which we reject the oppression produced by the capitalist system under which the bulk of the Latin American population lives. That stance conditions our "doing theology," and our reading of the Bible, turning it into a reading aimed at establishing justice on our continent and in our world. It is a committed reading, on the side of the poor and oppressed.

We have become more and more aware of the suffering and struggle of the women of our continent, especially of the poorest, those who are ranked third or fourth in the cruel categorization of the class system in which we live. Not all of them are saints; they are not pure, but they are people who beget and sustain life in the midst of the trash produced by what is supposed to be "civilization." We have paid attention to their problems, especially to their religious experience and the questions they raise. We have paid attention to the insights that emerge from their reflection on life and on God. All this has led us to take on as our mission the theological task of explaining and developing the faith, but doing so from a women's slant. Hence our reading of the Bible is tinted with our subjective/objective problems and the problems of the poor women with whom we have received the grace of sharing experience and the grace of getting to know them. Many things we have seen in the Bible, in the life of Mary, in the life of the people symbolized by Mary, take their inspiration from this common ground of the life of women of Latin America and from the lives of all the oppressed of our continent.

The aim of our biblical and theological reading is to open up space in society and in the churches so that the various religious experiences of women can be expressed from what they actually experience and intuit. Our intention in this reading is not necessarily to put women in a privileged position, but we do always bring out the way religious reality is experienced by women, since it is two women who are doing the thinking—with our differing life experiences, our different "states of life" (one lay, the other religious), and therefore with our different theological and literary styles.

Having established these initial points about our hermeneutics, we now begin to go through the New Testament in order to rediscover the countenance of Mary speaking to us and to our age. For our hermeneutics is dialogical, entering into conversation with the texts, a conversation charged with life and seeking paths for this life, in which men and women alike are called to proclaim the good news of God's Kingdom.

In this sense, the aim of our hermeneutics is not simply to understand the texts of the past and the story they tell as an example; our aim is also to understand and reactivate the past for the sake of today's liberation struggles. The Spirit of God is in us, and the Spirit's creativity, liberty, justice, and love are forever.

CHAPTER III

Mary in Scripture

1. MARIAN THEOLOGY AND GOD'S KINGDOM

The idea of the Kingdom of God is central for a Marian theology that is set within in a particular time and place and elaborated so as to validate woman as much as man, and it is the basis for a new way of approaching Mary's role in the history of our faith.

The idea of the Kingdom of God ties the various aspects of Christian theology together. It is an all-embracing concept, insofar as it includes God's deeds on behalf of men and women throughout the ages, deeds that are signs of the saving activity of this same God in the history of humankind. It is an open-ended concept insofar as it makes it possible to encompass activities that serve life beyond institutional boundaries and beyond what has already been established.

The idea of the Kingdom of God easily unfolds into the reign of life, of "life in abundance"; and all, men and women, young people, older people and children, contribute to making life happen, whether or not they are aware of their contribution.

This development we are making of the idea of the Kingdom of God goes beyond the person of Jesus. It extends to the whole of his movement in which men and women were active participants. We know that various groups within first-century Judaism were concerned about the question of the Kingdom and they gave differing answers to the question, "What do you have to do to enter the Kingdom of Heaven?" The Jesus movement held that the Kingdom was present in the midst of the poor, those who for various reasons were excluded by the purity requirements of the Judaic law. So sick people, tax collectors and prostitutes, social groups outside the code of Judaic holiness and hence "Godless" in legalistic terms, felt welcomed, "cured," and loved in the Jesus movement.

It is important that we take note that Jesus insists not on his own person but on God's concrete action, on the signs of the Kingdom, and that these take place with no political, cultural, or gender limits. This makes the concept of the Kingdom of God essential for Marian theology. It can provide the basis for reading Mary's actions in the various images she assumes in scripture and tradition, as well as in particular traditions, as actions that bring signs of the reign of God to the fore, concrete actions that make the presence of salvation in human history manifest.

Through their individual and collective action Mary/woman and Mary/people express new realities, realities that break into the ordinariness of sin, into the monotonous parade of injustices, into the habitual insensitivity to pain, into corruption clad in gold, into lies masquerading as truth. This new element reaches down into the depth of the human, a depth said to be from God, and there within us touches a desire for a new reality to spring forth like a flower from the ordinariness of our experience; it touches a desire for the Kingdom. The Kingdom happens. It has no preestablished moment; nor does it exist permanently in any movement or institution. It is like the breeze or Spirit that blows where it will, provided certain conditions be respected, even though those who are touched by it may be unaware of its presence.

The Kingdom, or better, its signs, have occurred, do occur, and will occur. The Kingdom is part of the gracious core of the fabric of our humanity; it is present in the precious pearl that few find, in the coin that few bother to look for, in the birds in the sky that few pause to contemplate, in the shared bread whose wonderful taste few pause to savor, in the wine drunk from a common cup that few allow to inebriate them, in the perfume of purest nard that few allow to be poured, in the love expressed in the foot-washing that few allow themselves to feel, and in so many other signs that only the little ones, the non-sages of this world, have tasted, have groped for; it is they who have intuited the mystery present in these signs, in these actions of love.

The Kingdom is a tender shoot, a frail mustard seed, the insignificant alms, the widow's mite, the tear for a dead-and-risen child, a cure for the fever, the chat beside a well, affection shown to children; the Kingdom is the presence of the gratui-tous, of the gift, of God's absolute gratuitousness. We believe in the presence of the Kingdom, right now, here in our midst, in the midst of so many kinds of dominations, protected by ar-mies of a thousand devils dressed up like winged cherubim or seraphim, armed and computerized.

We are speaking of the Kingdom in order to speak about Mary. We are speaking of the Kingdom that comes from her hands, from her womb, from her service. But when we speak of the Kingdom, the anti-Kingdom always makes its appearance, as though to remind us that what is human is always mixed, as though to indicate how true it is that impurity and impiety are mixed with mythical dreams of what is pure and pious.

It is in this mix that the extraordinary signs of the Kingdom take place; extraordinary because they are within the ordinari-ness of life, and extraordinary because they can be bearers of positive energy for building life. The Kingdom is the extraordi-nary within the ordinariness of life; it is help given to the preg-nant cousin, the glass of water to the thirsty person, clothing to the naked, caring for someone fallen along the road. These are common images of life, with no extraordinary significance for ordinary interpretation. But as interpreted by those who are reborn of God in the midst of the human race, these images are of the divine, of the extraordinary, because they can stir some-thing deep inside human beings and undo their selfishness and propel them toward the other, toward the transcendence that the other represents. Breaking the prisoner's chains is actually an act outside oneself, one that entails change, transforming a situation, re-establishing, or attempting to re-establish, justice. It also entails an internal revolution in those who have a passion for something besides themselves and the extension of themselves in their possessions. It entails leaving oneself, being able to go out to the needs of the other, without masking one's own needs in the needs of the other. That is why Luke likes to say that Mary did these things in a hurry, as though she could not lose a moment, as though the moment of love were unique, evanescent, impermanent in frail and fleeting human existence.

Mary announces the Kingdom, like Jesus and so many other men and women. Every action of Mary, of Jesus, of the prophets, apostles, disciples, male and female, converges toward the Kingdom, toward this way of being reborn in the midst of the old human race. It is so hard to be reborn. Nicodemus's question to Jesus often resounds in our ears, "How can a man be born again once he is old? . . . Can he return to his mother's womb and be born over again?" (John 3:4). From the viewpoint of the Kingdom, men and women can always be born again, they can always generate and be generated, provided they also generate a world of justice, a world of true sisters and brothers.

It is from the viewpoint of the Kingdom of God, of its signs in our history, that we can sketch out a different Marian theology. Yes, Marian theology, because the evangelists had nothing else in mind than to express God's activity in the midst of human events through Mary and Jesus. Mary speaks to us of God, of the divinity experienced by woman; she speaks of the Son of God who is born of the people and of the woman; she also speaks about the relationship among the woman, the child, the Spirit, and God.

Those who are reborn of God in the midst of the human race can beget works of justice and beauty; they can have a merciful heart and look at the world with love and tenderness. They are stamped with passion for what is human, passion that can change the life of groups, and of whole peoples. The passion for the Kingdom is a frail passion, as human existence is likewise frail. That is why one life is not enough to exhaust it. That is why the passion of the prophets, Mary, Jesus, and the just of all ages is not enough. With each new generation and at every moment of life, this passion is reborn; it is immortal flame; it is blood poured out, it is ever the same human-divine mystery.

To situate Mary in the perspective of the Kingdom of God is the only way to do theology rightly. To do theology rightly is also to express God's revelation and salvation in all that is human — man and woman. If God speaks to us and saves us in many ways, God speaks to us and saves us through the male and female realities that make up the human. Thus to do theology rightly is tenderly to touch the mystery of divinity present in man and in woman. It also means changing somewhat a hierarchy of patriarchal values that has left a strong imprint on our theology and our churches. When a patriarchal cultural world is the starting point, women are always subordinate to men, helpers, assistants, followers, or they are simply out of sight, nameless in history. They are not independent and are not even considered complementary. Everything happens as though the world were primarily made up of men and as though the "exemplary world" were that of men. Human salvation seems to have only one road, the one men have built, and all — men and women — must identify with a single model of perfection, the masculine one. This vision is unquestionably supported by dualist and one-dimensional anthropology, as we have already said.

Approaching theology on the basis of a Kingdom perspective opens ways that show greater respect for the complexity and complementarity of the two great elements that make up human reality. We all share in the Kingdom, though in different and complementary manners. To do a Marian theology on the basis of the Kingdom is to express a reality as mystery that eludes what can be objectively checked and concretely touched. It means affirming that God's salvation and creation have always shown themselves to be inseparably present in man and woman. Hence, it is not a part of God that saves — God as a whole saves us. Similarly, there is not a part of the human that saves another part or that is the single instrument of salvation, but rather it is the whole human that is saved and that is instrument of salvation.

This perspective highlights something essential in Christian faith, namely that God is our only savior and that we will be all in God. The patriarchal coloring or the values proper to a particular historical and cultural context are, and will be, less prominent in our reflection, so that other colors that reveal the marvels of being human may shine and may be seen in the light of a sun that indeed shines for all.

If that is so, to do Marian theology starting from the Kingdom does not mean simply speaking of a female figure as opposed to a male figure or to draw out God's revelation in the woman Mary and in women as a whole so as to show that they are also important. Basically it means trying to reveal something of the total human reality in its varied multiplicity and riches. The point of Marian theology is not to recite the "wonders" of Mary, or to show how we must love her more and more because she merits our love, but rather the point is to show that without her, without the dimension she represents, one half of us is missing, a half of humanity and hence a half of divinity, since human beings are the image of God.

We cannot do Marian theology on the basis of God's Kingdom simply in connection with Christology and in a way that would dilute what is specific to the female way of living and proclaiming the Kingdom. Mariology and Christology are ways of expressing the newness, always poetic, never pre-established, of the gentleness and justice that take place in the woman and the man who seek to love beyond their own limits.

Marian theology on the basis of the Kingdom also enables us to recognize Mary's "passion" for the poor, Mary's "passion" for God's justice, and thus to recover the power of the Spirit acting in women of all ages, even if written history has little to say about this activity. It means recovering the "dangerous memory" or "subversive memory" that can change things for it "not only keeps alive the suffering and hopes of Christian women in the past but also allows for a universal solidarity of sisterhood with all women of the past, present, and future who follow the same vision."[1] With this new vision as our starting point we cannot limit Mary to being the enchanting mother of Jesus, for she is, above all else, a "worker" in the harvest of the Kingdom, an active member of the movement of the poor, as is Jesus of Nazareth.

Mary's presence in the midst of peoples who struggle today for their liberation, especially in Latin America, helps us break away from a limited version of her past, that is, a version in which she is submissive to her Son, an expression of the submission of women to the established order of the prevailing patriarchal system. The liberation struggles of peoples broaden our horizon so that Mary becomes part of those who see a new light shining from Nazareth, symbol of the remote and uninfluential areas of the world.

Hope for the Kingdom of God is hope for deep human fulfillment; it is yearning for the unlimited within the bounds of human history. The Kingdom of God—made possible by the creative power of the Spirit—is building, rebuilding, beginning anew, rebirth, resurrection. Human beings quickly become old. They get tired, lose their strength, become disillusioned. That is why they have to begin again. Each man and each woman, each generation and each people has to be reborn and begin anew. Thus there is infinite human yearning for God, the ever new, eternal youth, what is beyond the world of the senses. . . .

The theology that speaks of the Kingdom of God speaks symbolically of the Kingdom of yearning for the unlimited in its many forms. This is the Kingdom of the perfect man, perfect woman, perfect world, and perfect God—the man, woman, world, and God of our yearning. Hence from the angle of the Kingdom we can sing with Mary, "He has deposed the powerful from their thrones and has raised up the lowly. . . ." This is the song of the continual battle in history of the lowly ones confronting the seat of absolute power that tortures and inebriates many and prevents the hungry from "being filled with good things. . . ."[2] This was the battle of women of the Old and New Testaments who were intimately connected to the life and hope of their people.

2. THE TRADITION OF WOMEN WHO BEGET THE PEOPLE

Within its own culture, the patriarchal world has generated a series of values which, almost in reaction to the exaggerated evaluation of what is male, has manifested the essential presence of the female dimension. To begin with, on the symbolic horizon this means that the figure of woman is linked to the life of the human race, linked to the life of the people, to its continuity. This role of women has always remained basic and irreplaceable. In scripture men's battle against different oppressors of the people or the struggle against various nations or invaders apparently does not provide the only image for expressing the people's life and resistance. Even if the male aspect of struggle and combat seems to prevail, here and there it is clear that the male aspect does not stand by itself and that alone it does not generate or sustain life.

Even in Genesis, Adam calls his wife Eve, that is, "the mother of the living" (Gen. 3:20). Thus, the figure of woman is a vital component and has a collective aspect — the figure of woman expresses not only an individual figure but is the expression of the face of the people. This does not mean that woman alone is the figure of the people to the exclusion of man. Both are that figure, but in different and complementary manners.

Our particular concern at this point is to recognize how certain symbolisms in scripture accumulate around the woman figure so as to express woman's reality which centuries of patriarchy have obscured. Hermeneutically speaking, it is very important to take the biblical figures in both their personal and collective aspects. This means that although a particular account may emphasize more the action of one personality and may revolve around a main protagonist, we must recognize that this is a literary procedure with a specific catechetical or historical purpose and moreover that in actuality heroes and heroines never act alone. In their own action they are bearing the often silent action of many people. Hence the victory of a hero or heroine is always the victory of a people or the victory of a group. Similarly when something new or different comes on the scene it is the experience of a group and not of an individual in isolation. To read the scriptures from this angle is to perceive that what is narrated refers to a body, to a people, and not to individual quasi-gods with superhuman powers. No doubt some persons rise above the mass, and have particular, even very special, tasks, but their actions take place in a connected whole which makes the resulting effect or consequences possible.

Limiting our reflection to the women in the Bible, we find that the figures of Miriam, Hannah, Ruth, Judith, Esther, and others are both images of women and images of a people. Whatever is the truth of their existence in history, these women perform extraordinary actions that can save the people in different ways and in varied situations. Their actions reveal the power of

God saving the people. The same thing could be said about male figures, although in a different fashion.

Miriam, a prophetess and Moses' sister, picks up the tambourine and, leading many women, dances and praises the Lord who has saved the Jews by leading them across the sea with dry feet. Miriam represents women and people able to give thanks after a concrete experience of salvation.

Ruth symbolizes the people as small and even on the point of vanishing but ultimately surviving through the continuity of generation and the security that there will be descendants.

Judith defeats the oppressor of the people by using her feminine physical attributes. God makes her more beautiful and attractive, her charms become even more surpassing, and she succeeds in cutting off the enemy's head. The book of Judith is a parable of the victory of a frail people symbolized in the figure of woman.

Esther becomes queen and saves the Jews through her intervention. Once more we find the image of the woman who saves the people or the people saved in the figure of woman, symbolizing God's ongoing activity in the midst of human history.

Hannah, the sterile wife of Elkanah, gives birth to the judge Samuel, who from an early age is set aside to serve God and the people. Hannah is woman but she is also the people that can beget its own servants who are likewise servants of the Lord.

To read the life and action of outstanding figures in the Bible from both a personal and collective angle is to restore to the biblical accounts the power of history which occurs not only through isolated individuals even if the story is told especially around them. The edifying and heroic stories centered on one personality must be brought back down to the precarious and interdependent reality of human history. History is not the story of great men and great women but a weaving of many interconnected threads of different colors. To reduce human-divine history to a history made up basically of heroes is to introduce an anthropological vision marked by the presence of supermen, and to some extent of superwomen. Such a vision, however, would make the activity of countless thousands of human beings secondary and ineffective and furthermore it would reduce the responsibility for history, which really belongs to all, to a few who would bear it on behalf of most of the human race. Given the spirit of our age, it is archaic and backward to emphasize heroes and heroines. Such a procedure cannot take into account the progress of human awareness in various realms.

Therefore, without denying each person's mission and particularly those of people who have special charisms, our age more and more demands that we rediscover in the texture of human history, both past and present, the collective aspect of human activities: our building history together. Our own thinking here is based on, and develops out of, the anthropology at work in our reading of the biblical texts, especially those that express Mary's story most directly.

As we have seen in the previous chapters, the characteristic feature of this anthropology is that it seeks to see history in its unity, many-sidedness, and reality. It is an anthropology that goes beyond the limits of subjectivity and becomes increasingly intersubjective and cultural. All this enables us to tackle the question of the collective aspect of biblical figures, particularly women, in a way that is closer to the everyday reality of human life and to the thrust of social experience.

This effort also strives to bring the biblical story back down to its natural proportion in relation to other histories, even though that history is rooted in an original experience of God in which we have been shaped and out of which we live even today, imbibing its countless riches. Bringing it down to its natural size places the history of the ancient people of the Bible in a dialogical perspective in relation to the history of other peoples, seeing its figures no longer larger than life and no longer uncritically sacralizing them as "giants" or examples for other histories. Reducing biblical figures to natural size permits a more human approach to them, an approach within the relativity of our existence, our various conflicts and conquests. Such a procedure opens a space in which the history of women, who today in their striving for liberation are closely allied with all the poor and oppressed of the earth, can emerge and grow.

3. MARY IN SCRIPTURE: HEIR OF HER PEOPLE'S TRADITION AND RENEWER OF THEIR HOPE

We are going to try to understand the figure of Mary in the light of the history of biblical women who are images of the people, and in relation to the Kingdom of God, which is no longer limited to Israel but is announced to all peoples.

In the Old Testament, Yahweh creates the people and enters into the midst of the people of Israel as Savior (see Zephaniah). In the New Testament, the new people is born linked to the old, born out of the hopes of the old, but basically it "breaks forth" from God. Mary, image of the people that hopes, receives God in her womb or, in other words, the people becomes God's dwelling (*Shekinah*).

The recognition of Mary, image of the faithful people, as God's special dwelling is the highest expression of the mystery of the incarnation and the most original expression of the Christianity that takes shape out of the initial Jesus movement. The statement "God becomes flesh in Jesus" should be completed with another one that has the same theological import: "God is born of a woman." Both signify an extraordinary qualitative step or leap in the historic awareness of the relationship of humankind with God. The insight that God is no longer to be sought in strict observance of worship or in the letter of the law, but in the poorest of men and women, brings about among Jesus' followers a revolution whose consequences in history are still taking place. Our understanding of this mystery which touches the very structures of what makes us human has evolved slowly and gradually from the time of Jesus to our own time.

The incarnation is fundamentally the experience each woman and each man, sustained by a community of faith, has of God present in the frailty of human flesh. This means God is present in the other and in me and becomes an appeal for conversion of life in the other and in me.

Here again we are moving beyond the dualistic theological anthropology which sees the incarnation as taking place only in Jesus of Nazareth while we simply live and celebrate the mystery in him. If we replace this with a realist theological anthropology, God has then taken on the flesh of all humankind since creation. Knowledge of this magnificent fact, however, comes to mature expression only in the Jesus movement. This interpretation has clearly not been a constant in Christian tradition. We have moved from realism to idealism, passing through a series of different interpretations that sought to reconcile various aspects.

Such a perspective on the incarnation gives back to Mary her place in this process of the human maturation of the relationship with God, a place analogous to, though also different from, that of Jesus. It also enables us to see more forcefully the theological aim of the New Testament writers despite the different nuances in their accounts.

Here we should pay attention to the angel's words to Mary, "The Holy Spirit will come upon you and the power of the Most High will overshadow you" (Luke 1:35). What is referred to, what is underway, is the birth of the new people of God, which is going to restore God's justice. Hence, from the viewpoint of the New Testament's theological message, the new people is not born of a sexual relationship between a man and a woman. From such a relationship other men and women are born in a biological sense, but not the people of God, not the children of God, not the faithful servants of the Lord. This is a theological reading of the birth of an individual and of a people.

The children of God are the work of the Spirit of God. They are born not of the flesh, but of the Spirit. Hence, one can always be born again by being born of the Spirit, and one is born of the Spirit when one begins to take part in building a world of brothers and sisters (John 3:4).

This is just what Luke's text (1:34) is talking about; that is, about Mary, about the people, about Mary who is the image of the people made fruitful by the Spirit of God, from whom is born the new humankind, which will be woven out of all the nations of the earth. Mary is symbol of the people that she begets from God, and Jesus is symbol of the new people begotten of God. The name Jesus means "Yahweh saves," and indicates the presence of God's salvation in human flesh and in human history.

The early Christian community always associated Jesus' mission with Mary's. That is why it placed on Mary's lips the Magnificat (Luke 1:46–56), a song of God's victory over the powerful, a song of the liberation of the poor, and on Jesus' lips, the programmatic sermon of liberation given at the synagogue in Nazareth (Luke 4:16–21), which is taken from the prophet Isaiah. Both statements have the same theological import. They speak of the God who liberates, of the presence of God's Spirit in woman and man, the Spirit who can change human relations in accordance with the will of the Most High.

From this angle we cannot find anything in the New Testament texts that does not have a deep theological intention. The aim of the evangelists and other New Testament writers is to tell how God relates to humankind, how God revives the hope of the poor, how God's presence occurs in the midst of the events of history. Throughout the history of the church, however, due to the influence of many different cultures and in contact with different peoples, the great theological purpose of the New Testament has been forgotten and it has often been interpreted in accordance with religious traditions alien to Judeo-Christianity.

To some extent Mary, the great woman, image of the new people, has been relegated to second or third place. It became customary to speak of her more as an individual woman, especially favored by God, one who possesses all feminine attributes. People spoke of her mysterious relationship with Joseph; there was a proliferation of fairy-tale-like stories; speculation about her mysterious pregnancy increased; and finally there were stories about the mysterious birth of her son. Mary's life was separated from the life of the people, and that meant that there was no more collective theology; that is, Mary's connection to the collective event of the Kingdom of God breaking into history was no longer emphasized. From that point onward, what was produced was a pious biology or a pious physiology of the mysterious reality of Mary, with the accent more on the power of God over woman than on the saving and creative power of God in the midst of God's people.

To the extent that Mary's life was reduced to a handful of mysterious biological phenomena, questions about Mary's physical virginity multiplied, and that meant a turning away from the essential aspect she represents. Accenting the biological problem aggravated the tendency to bypass and even suppress sexuality, to regard it as something sinful, thereby further removing God's humanity. Hence, reading virginity in biological terms does not seem to do justice to God, who creates human beings in the wholeness of all their aspects, including sexuality.

The basic aim of the evangelists was not to do "theological

biology" or "pious biology" but theology, both in continuity with, and breaking away from, the ancient traditions of the Old Testament. The New Testament seeks to show that with Mary and Jesus there begins a new age for the history of humankind. A kind of qualitative leap in humankind's practice and religious consciousness takes place: the awareness that God is present in human flesh. God dwells on the human earth, has set up a tent in our midst, has fully taken on our sorrows and joys. God becomes human flesh and is discovered and loved in human flesh. This is the great new element of the New Testament, a newness that has serious consequences in history, as we have already said. Two thousand years after its proclamation we still hesitate to accept it, so deep is its content.

The powers of this world, including the religious powers, have domesticated, put the brakes on, and manipulated the great affirmation of Christian faith that God is found and loved in human flesh. Sometimes we seem to remain at an almost primitive religious stage in which the gods control human life independently of human consent and activity.

The New Testament, therefore, makes a theological re-reading of human-divine history. The sacred writers had no intention of copying models from Greco-Roman religion, which speak of gods marrying chosen women,[3] nor of insisting on the superiority of the vow of virginity over marriage, nor of treating the problems faced by a Jewish single mother, nor of presenting the power of a woman who does not need the presence of a man in her life. All these interpretations, which have developed within different Christian communities at different periods, to some extent represent a turning away, albeit unconscious, from the theological and catechetical aim present in the New Testament texts.

What the New Testament strives to say is that God's gesture of love is repeated again in Mary and in Jesus, or in other words, is repeated in humankind as a new creation. For the sacred writers this is the great moment in human history, the moment when the human being is recreated, when it is love rather than the law that prevails, the moment when we touch the depths of the human mystery, mystery and dwelling-place of God. As the book of Genesis speaks of humankind's beginning, utilizing the mythical figures of Adam and Eve, the religious-symbolic expression of a people recognizing its origins in God, the Gospels speak of the beginning of a new humankind, built up from those who are most outcast from all nations.

This new humankind is no longer represented by mythical beings, but by historic beings who live concrete events, suffer the contingencies of specific economic, political, and social situations. Christianity accentuates and makes privileged the historic dimension present in Judaism, and goes further than Judaism in thinking about God's transcendence on the basis of the limited reality of human beings.

Let us examine the situation of women in Mary's time, in order better to understand what the New Testament texts say about her.

4. WOMEN IN MARY'S TIME

When we speak about Mary, we must first of all keep in mind that we are thinking and talking about a woman. This woman lived in a time and place, in a particular context, set within family, social, economic, political, and religious structures. Therefore, we can shed light on the little we know about this woman and her story if we look closer at the context in which she lived, and if in addition we try to visualize the place or role of women in that context.

This becomes even more necessary if we take into account the theological perspective from which we have been taking our bearings from the outset: the Latin American viewpoint whose basic aim is to reflect on the mysteries of Christian faith starting from the social, economic, and cultural context of injustice and inequality in which the Christian people of our continent are sunk. Therefore the theology today being developed in Latin America regards the contextual element and the historical sources of theology as very important, without thereby ignoring the element of mystery and transcendence. On the contrary, the historical and structural element helps us perceive better the shape and particularities of God's revelation in a particular age, to a particular people, and to particular persons. That element is equally helpful to Christians and theologians today, enabling them to read the revelation of God's mystery within the social, economic, and political categories of our own age.

This is what we must do with Mary. In order to approach her person, her mystery, her figure-symbol, and what God wants to communicate to us through her, we must first situate better in her own context that young woman, Miriam of Nazareth, espoused to a just man named Joseph. Knowing this woman better means having a closer knowledge of the life of other women, her contemporaries: their ways and customs, their place and role in the family, in society, in the economic system, and in the religious structure of the people of Israel. For before, and besides, being the glorious queen that our faith venerates as Mother of God, Mary is the faithful Jewish woman, woman of her people and of her age, from whose fleshly womb was born the male son who was given the name Jesus. A look at the situation of women in Judaism before and during Mary's time will give us more data for pondering the mystery of this woman named Mary. The information we provide mainly illuminates a situation of patriarchal domination, although we are aware of breaks made in this by other tendencies and movements of the time.

According to the information we have in the Old Testament, an Israelite woman, from a juridical standpoint, was more *thing* than *person*.[4] Before marriage she was under her father's authority. At marriage she became the property of the man her father had chosen to be her husband. He had to *pay* the father a sum of money for her, that is, a *dowry*. If the husband died or the woman happened to be repudiated, she was placed under the guardianship of her eldest son or her original family, and if her husband had died she then had to wait to see if one of her husband's brothers wanted to marry her. In all respects the man was more her *owner* and *master* than husband or father (Gen. 3:16).

In relation to the Old Testament, later Judaism moved backward rather than forward, evidencing a virulent contempt for women. Rabbinic literature almost never uses the honorable title "daughter of Abraham" when speaking of women, but almost exclusively uses the equivalent "son of Abraham" for men. Its statements about women are belittling, saying for example that they eat too much, are curious, jealous, or fickle.[5] The woman walks at the head of funeral processions, but that is to indicate that she is responsible for the death that has occurred. Nevertheless, we should note that in the midst of all this misogyny in much of the Old Testament and Rabbinic literature, there stands the wisdom literature, which, while speaking harshly of the harm done by authoritarian women (Prov. 6:24; 7:5; 9:13; 11:22; 19:13; etc.; Ecclus. 25:16f.; 19:2; etc.), praises the "virtuous woman" with enthusiasm (Prov. 12:4; 18:22; 31:10–31; Ecclus. 36:27f.; 26:13f.). She is, however, always present in connection with her husband: "Like the sun rising in the Lord's heavens, the beauty of a virtuous wife shines in the house organized around her husband" (Ecclus. 26:16).

In the world Mary lived in woman's inferior nature was indicated by her *bodiliness*. The female body bore various condemnations that made it inferior and confined it to a subordinate condition:

—being the bearer of sin and the reason it had entered into the world. In Genesis 3 the original fall of the human race and the consequent fault that spreads to all humankind are attributed to the initiative of the woman, thus bringing upon her the idea that she is an inferior being, subject to passions, and so forth;

—having its monthly biological cycle regarded as impurity. During their menstrual period, women could not cook for pious Jews, and any place, person, or object they might touch, step on, or sit on automatically became impure;[6]

—having no value in itself, but only as the vessel for the reproduction of male seed. Woman's body had no value in itself, as her way of being present and communicating in the world, but it was always related to reproduction and conception. Hence, virginity, widowhood, and sterility were regarded as a divine curse. Further, women without male children were regarded as inferior to those who had given birth to males. Sterility was always blamed on the woman and never on the man.

Women were as excluded and relegated to second place *in the family* as they were in public life. Their education was limited to learning how to do housework, sewing, spinning, and taking care of younger brothers and sisters. Toward the father they "certainly had the same duties as the sons, to give him food and drink, to clothe and cover him, to help him in and out when he grew old, and to wash his face, hands, and feet. But they did not have the same rights to succession and inheritance as the male children."[7] The father had the right to sell his daughter as a slave until she reached the age of twelve and a half. And up to that age she had no right to refuse the husband the father chose for her. Her engagement was often a source of income for the father, who received a dowry from the groom.[8] So there was not much difference between "acquiring" women and slaves.[9]

After marriage the woman had the right to be supported by her husband, and she could go to court to demand that the right be fulfilled. For her part she had to obey him as her lord, and such obedience became a religious duty. Indeed, the husband could demand that the wife make vows of obedience to him, although the woman could go to court when such vows put her in a discreditable situation.[10] While the woman was bound to observe marital fidelity, the man was prohibited only from committing adultery with married women. Since polygamy was allowed, the wife had to put up with having concubines around, and if they were more favored than she in terms of offspring, they had more prestige.[11]

The right to divorce was all on the side of the man; the woman had only the right to request a legal annulment when offenses or deep disrespect for her were such that they placed her in an unworthy situation. As alluded to above, as a widow a woman remained tied to her husband — that is, to his family — if he died without leaving sons. In such a situation, the widow had to wait — without making any overtures at all — for the brothers of the dead husband to contract levirate marriage with her or to let her know that they would not. Otherwise, she could not remarry. Hence, the woman's familial dependence on the man went beyond the bounds of death.

The woman's situation in *social, economic, and political* matters was no different. A woman did not take part in public life. When she left her house, she had to keep her face and her head hidden with a veil. If she did not, her failure to observe correct behavior was such that her husband had the right to get rid of

her without paying the amount stipulated in the marriage contract. Thus, in public, women had to be invisible. The rules of
decorum forbade a man to be alone with a woman, to look at a
married woman, and even to pay her a compliment. For a Jew
of high standing in society, such as a scribe or even one studying
to be a scribe, it was a shameful thing to talk with a woman in
the street.

Before marrying, young women from leading families were
accustomed to staying within the house; in some locations the
limit for married women of means was extended only to the
entrance to the courtyard of her house.[12] For economic reasons,
women of the popular classes could not live in complete retire-
ment like those of the upper class. Since they had to help their
husbands, they were obliged to work in the fields and in trade.
A woman working in the fields alone was viewed as negatively
as a man chatting with a strange woman.

A characteristic indication of the traditional place of women
in Eastern cultures and in Jewish society in particular is the
prayer of a man thanking God for not making him an infidel,
uneducated, a slave, or a woman.[13] This expression indicates the
very low condition of women not only within Judaism but in the
whole Eastern world.

In *religious affairs,* woman's situation was not much different.
Worship, an essential element in the Jewish nation, was entirely
in the hands of men. Women did not even have the right to go
into the more sacred parts of the temple, and they could not
take part in the celebrations as priestesses. During the cere-
monies of sanctification, they remained along the sides of the
temple, never in the middle. Their place was far from the altar,
and that fact symbolized their real place in society. The more
radically the priestly tradition prevailed in Jewish religion, the
more the women were excluded. That may reflect an abhorrence
of a memory of the sacred prostitution in pagan worship, thus
prompting the legislators of the Israelite priestly code to keep
women separate from worship and the temple.[14]

Despite the great women figures singled out by the scriptures
(noted in section 2 of this chapter), whose role in the history of
the covenant of the people with their God was essential — Miriam, Huldah, Esther — access to the temple and the liturgy was

never opened to women. The fact that God was represented as a being with male, not with female, features certainly played a role. A direct consequence was the fact that male domination over women was regarded as a divine right and approaching divinity was seen as a male privilege.

With Pharisaism and the consequent decentralizing of the life of temple piety, women found new openings and possibilities. Emphasis now fell not so much on worship as on the regulations for ritual purity (eating, and so forth) which were observed outside the temple space. Since women had to prepare meals according to religious prescriptions, they had a little bit of power, namely that of safeguarding sanctification. Although they became men's equal with regard to observing prescriptions and prohibitions, nevertheless the blemish of impurity weighing on their bodies and their menstrual cycles periodically took them away from these functions in which they played an important role in the religious observance of their faith.

Moreover, women were excused from studying the Torah and even advised not to, since they would only be able to put it to bad use. At a very early period, it seems that women were called to read the Torah, but by Tannaitic times, this custom no longer existed. They were also forbidden to teach.[15] A woman could not give witness, teach her children, or recite the table prayer. She had a special place in the synagogue, behind the railing. In religious legislation her situation was equivalent to that of pagan slaves and younger children. Her freedom for divine service was thus limited, and in religious terms she stood on a lower level than man.

This was the social, economic, political, cultural, and religious context into which the woman Miriam was born in Nazareth of Galilee. The glimpses the Gospels give us of this Jewish woman show her first as a very young woman dealing with an unexpected pregnancy; then as a mature mother of an adult man, accompanying him on his way as he is agitating the masses; and then as a woman who remained united to the group of her son's followers after his death.

Unfolding in this context that we have attempted to describe, Mary's daily life must have been not very different externally from that of any other wife and mother of her age; caring for her house and her son took up all her time. Her interior life is set in the religious pattern of a Jewish woman of her time: very much turned inward, with far less visibility than the religious life of men. Although they were also obliged to observe the commandments, women were dispensed from all those commandments whose observance was tied to particular hours of the day so they could fulfill their material duties (nursing babies, and so forth).

Probably a member of a humble family, Mary was a woman of a small town. Then as now that indicated a sharp difference. The life of women in a big city like Jerusalem was quite different from the life of women from towns of the interior like Nazareth. In Jerusalem, in the shadow of the temple, in an atmosphere where the experts in the law were present, women were also affected and picked up something of the teaching of the sages and their reflections on the word of God. That was harder in the provincial regions. Nevertheless, from the scanty information we have on Mary's life, we can deduce that she was not completely disconnected from Jerusalem. According to data in the Gospels, she had family ties to levite circles, and furthermore she was related to the dynasty of the house of David.[16]

In addition, Mary is a figure who bridges both Testaments. She experienced what it meant to be a woman in Old Testament and rabbinic Judaism, and she also shared in and savored the taste of the good news about women brought by Jesus her son.

While the Baptist preached to women and baptized them (see Matt. 21:32), Jesus went further: he began an equal discipleship of men and women, and there were women in his group "following" and "serving" him. Among these women the Gospels often mention Mary (see Luke 8:1–3; John 19:25; etc.). Jesus not only raised women above the level at which custom kept them, but as savior sent to all (Luke 7:36–50), he put them on the same level as men (Matt. 21:31–32) in the new community of the Kingdom of God.[17]

Mary took part in and tasted this new liberating community experience in her being as a woman and in the connection she maintained with the movement started by her son. Without ceasing to live the great experiential wealth of Judaism and of her people's reflection on their faith, she, along with the women of the first moment of the church, was bearer of a new hope and a new way of being woman. In contrast to the gnostic currents of that time (Acts 13:50; 17:4, 12; 2 Tim 3:6; etc.), Christian preaching won over women from the beginning (Acts 16:13ff.; 17:4, 12, 34; 18:18), and they called each other "sisters" (*adelphē*) as the men called each other "brothers" (*adelphoi:* see Rom. 16:1; 1 Cor. 9:5ff.). In Christianity women were not only objects but agents of religion and charitable activity (Acts 9:36ff.). Paul himself, who is so contradictory in his statements about women (see Gal. 3:28 vs. 2 Cor. 11:3; 1 Cor. 11:3, 7), never tires in his praise for those women who "wear themselves out" in the Lord so the church may grow (Rom. 16:6, 12f.). Unlike Judaism, early Christianity's initiation rite was not exclusive and opened up for women a new and unexpected era of participation and communion.[18]

This information is very important for the Marian theology we are attempting to do. In the church we have often seen a kind of preaching and devotion to Mary that are really more Judaic than Christian. When Mary is presented as the prototype of the mild and self-effacing woman, who is passive and agreeable and always says "yes," we are no doubt very close to the picture of the Jewish woman we sought to describe above, but we are certainly not realizing and assimilating all the newness introduced by Christianity.

As legitimate representative of the people of Israel, figure-symbol of faithful Zion, Mary is also nothing less than the bearer of the new Israel, the new people, the new covenant that God is contracting with humankind, the new enterprise of the Kingdom of God. In this new enterprise, in this new covenant, women are no longer seen as passive and submissive to men, no longer as inferior beings in the social, economic, political, and religious spheres. Rather they are seen as active and responsible agents, men's companions, taking on side-by-side with men many of the tasks that are part of announcing the good news.

The New Testament reflects this newness when it presents the group of women who followed Jesus, the first women converts, and also the person of Mary, at the heart of the early community. The Mary who appears in the Gospels is a woman

whose bodiliness, speech, and social position challenge established patterns; the elements highlighted in the New Testament's understanding of Mary are thus very different from those
which have been put forth in traditional piety's view of Mary
and which have led generations of Christians to venerate her as
that humble and obedient woman, submissive to men and to the
structures of her time. It is the former, the Mary of the Gospels,
on whose lips is placed the Magnificat, God's program for the
messianic era; it is that Mary who does not hesitate to leave her
house or to contradict her son (see Mark 3:31–55), who remains
at the foot of the cross to the end and in community with the
emerging church; it is that Mary who is seen as a colleague,
reference point, and symbol by women from around the world
who are rediscovering that they have their own identity and a
mission in society and church.

With these reflections as our starting point we will now go
on to read the New Testament texts.

5. MARY IN THE NEW TESTAMENT

(a) "Born of a Woman . . .": Paul's Marian Theology

The oldest Christian witness to Mary in the New Testament
is found in Paul's letter to the Galatians.[19] Before taking up the
key text in Galatians we should first quickly mention 1:19, which
speaks of "James, the brother of the Lord," from which one can
neither conclude much about whether this James might be another son of Mary[20] nor determine much about Paul's intention
in mentioning him. We mention the text here only because it
has a slight bearing on matters discussed later in this book. We
can now move on to chapter 4, verse 4, which is more important
for us.

The context is Paul's defense in chapters 3 and 4 of the thesis
he puts forth in chapter 2 about justification by faith and not
through the law. He contrasts the situation of human beings
under the law and under faith: "Before faith came, we were
allowed no freedom by the law; we were being looked after till
faith was revealed" (3:23). According to Paul, this idea was revealed with the sending of the Son to justify those who believe

in him and to assure them that they are true adoptive children and heirs. This is how Paul begins to describe this new state of things: "When the fullness of time had come, God sent forth his son, born of a woman, born under the law, to deliver from the law those who were subjected to it, so that we might receive our status as adopted sons" (Gal. 4:4–5). Paul here makes the mystery of the incarnation of the Son of God the central axis, the "fullness," around which history hinges, announcing—more than a new age for humankind—a new humankind that none other than God takes on as adopted sons and daughters.

Paul's language in these verses—specifically with regard to Mary—although tangential and indirect, nevertheless places her at the very center where this new humankind is being generated. The "fullness of time" that the apostle mentions is both end and beginning: it is the end of a journey during which God led God's people, a journey of God's self-revelation, God speaking to the people "in fragmentary and diverse ways"; it is the beginning of a new state of things in which God takes human flesh and a human face within history, in the midst of a people, of which the woman Mary is the faithful figure. The people of Israel and humankind are again born from the womb of a woman, moving from childhood to adulthood, really becoming "children of God" (Gal. 4:1–7).[21]

The phrase "born of a woman" is a common expression in Judaism used to indicate the human condition of an individual. There are parallel expressions in the Old Testament (see Job 14:1; 15:14; 25:4) as well as in other places in the New Testament (Matt. 11:11; Luke 7:28) where it is applied to other biblical figures besides Jesus. So its use here is no authority for trying to uncover Paul's intention in order to draw out more or less explicit references to Mary's virginity or motherhood. However, with the freedom the Spirit grants us for interpreting God's word, we can strive to reflect theologically on the greater mystery that Jesus' birth through Mary's fruitful womb is intended to reveal to us.

The Marian theology in Galatians 4:4 presents a potential for convergence. In the figure of the woman who gives birth to the Son of God in the fullness of time eschatology and history, anthropology and theology converge. It is the very miracle of life and the life process, decisively marked by God, which bears the sign of this convergence. The Word of God, the Son pre-existing since before the foundation of the world, takes flesh in the person of Jesus of Nazareth. This process, which is at once very simple biologically and is yet so miraculously transcendent, takes place through the mediation of woman. It is she—the "woman"—who forms, of her own flesh and blood, the flesh and blood that will be recognized as the person of God's very self walking on the paths of history.

We might say that from this moment onward we can speak of anthropocentric theology and theocentric anthropology—from this moment onward begins the "fullness of time" when God becomes human born of a woman, when God takes flesh of man and woman, when man and woman are finally, definitively, the fullness of creation and fully the image of the One who created them. From this point onward there is no more room for male-centeredness or any kind of dualism, since any kind of anthropological or theological reductionism cedes to the confession of faith that the Word became flesh in human flesh, flesh of man and woman, in the actuality of history and within its limits.

Moreover, in the Marian theology of this verse, there is a convergence of the plural and singular, of the personal and collective dimensions of the love story taking place between God and humankind. To say that the time has come to its fullness because God has sent his son "born of a woman" is to speak of new creation. Creation, from which time originates, springs from the loving heart of God who initiates life and history out of the previous chaos; it is the explosion of life under the breath of God's Spirit. God's own definitive entry into this creation, through woman's flesh, sets in motion a new and full age: a new creation, where God's Creator Spirit makes all things new, making virgins pregnant and setting worlds in motion, tumbling the powerful and raising up the lowly, filling the hungry and despoiling the rich. From the body of a woman who is an individual—Mary of Nazareth—but who is also a figure of the people—faithful Zion, chosen and ardently loved as wife—the Spirit's covenant with human history and flesh prompts the breakthrough of the new people, the new Israel, Jesus Christ. Being herself of the faithful people, the new people, begotten by God's Spirit in the flesh of man and woman, Mary is the new ark of the covenant between God and humankind, the poor and limited humankind that is continually transfigured through the glory of Yahweh.

Finally in the Marian theology of this verse there is a convergence between the many and varied dimensions of the Kingdom of God which is effected in the incarnation of Jesus in Mary's womb. If in the Gospels Jesus speaks of the Kingdom as the historic aim of the one God, whom he announces, it is just as clear that this Kingdom is realized, in all its intensity and manifest truth, in his own person. This small verse of Paul's in his letter to the Galatians tells us more: the Kingdom has arrived, the fullness of time is here, the new creation is now a reality because God has sent God's son, born of a woman. Starting from the light of this mystery, therefore, the Kingdom takes place in the community of men and women who with their struggles and sufferings, sorrows and joys, are at every moment making the untiring and beautiful newness of love explode. The Kingdom, which is the perfect realization of our yearning as children of God, is put within range of our sight and within reach of our hands, already, here and now, through God become the man Jesus in the flesh of the woman Mary.

(b) Mary, Spouse of the Earlier People: Matthew's Original Intuition

The evangelist Matthew is addressing a Christianized Jewish community. Hence his particular concern is to retrieve the founding events of Judaism and situate them in the light of the Jesus event, sign of the presence of God's Kingdom. Everything a faithful Jew was hoping for is taking place in this new age. Matthew reads the "new events" brought about by the action of Jesus and of the community of his followers as the fulfillment of the promises made by Yahweh to Israel. The only difference is that the fulfillment of the promises now goes beyond the limits of a people in order to reach all peoples, calling them to true life.

Matthew begins his Gospel with the genealogy of Jesus. "Jacob was the father of Joseph the husband of Mary. It was of her that Jesus who is called the Messiah was born" (Matt. 1:16). Jesus' lineage is that of the ancient Jewish people, the people that began with Abraham, with Jacob, going by way of Tamar, Rahab, and Ruth (1:3, 5), and which went through a long history of faithfulness and unfaithfulness to the Lord of life. After recalling many ancestors, Matthew comes to Joseph, husband of Mary, of whom "Jesus . . . was born." In symbolic language, Mary, of whom the Messiah is born, is "wife" of the whole old people, out of which emerges the new people, and hence the former people is linked to something unfinished. It is interesting to note that the genealogy is Joseph's. Mary is the virgin wife, the open-ended newness linked to a people with a long tradition. Old and new are united and again beget the faithful people. This is the dynamic of the God of the Bible which reappears now with a wider horizon because it is more universal and not restricted to a single people. On other occasions the Old Testament people experienced God's saving presence in different manners. Now they experience it again and what is experienced is subsequently written down with an extraordinary set of symbols, marriage symbolism that can reach down to the roots of the human and can mobilize humanity because it beckons toward the mystery of our existence.

Hence, "it is by the Holy Spirit that she has conceived . . ." (1:20). One notes a kind of "break" in the genealogy, since the only thing said about the mother, Mary, is that she is the wife of Joseph. However, her partner, her mate in the begetting of the Messiah, is someone else. The begettor, or better, the partner in generating the Messiah, hope of peoples, is the Holy Spirit, God's Spirit.

The Messiah comes from the people and comes from God. He is the new symbol of the covenant that recurs in the image of nuptials. Matthew's theological intention seems clear, despite the biologizing intepetations his text has received. The point here is the birth of the new people of God, begotten in the woman who is the figure of the people.

God's Spirit comes over the woman, as in the creation text (Gen. 1:2) where God's Spirit hovers over the waters and makes them fruitful. Thus it is the Spirit who engenders in the people the people of God, the people that will continue to proclaim justice and righteousness over the face of the earth.

According to Matthew's theology, this all takes place in order to fulfill the word of the prophet Isaiah (Isa. 7:14), re-read in light of the new things happening among Jews and pagans. The virgin will give birth to a son who will be called Emmanuel, "God with us." The great new element is that this "God with us" can be recognized in human flesh for God is begotten in human flesh by the Spirit of God. Hence, Mary has given birth even though Joseph "had no relations with her. . . ."

Joseph is the quintessence of the ancient people and the early Jewish tradition, and he recognizes the Messiah despite doubts and difficulties. He is the "man of good will" and he is able to accept the newness that represents a turning point in early Judaism, the end of one wait so as to await other, more expansive things in which all the peoples of the earth can share.

Joseph's love for his wife reminds us of the love of Hosea for his wife who prostitutes herself, a symbol of the love of God who is always pursuing God's loved one. There is in Matthew's text, however, one great difference. Here the woman is the symbol of the faithful people out of which the Messiah is born, and Joseph is the former people which to some extent has turned away from the covenant and which is again called to a new wedding so that love may begin anew. Hence, he does not reject her, and he recognizes the depth of what is happening within the people. Joseph is the faithful Jew who accepts the newness of the Messiah; Joseph is the people for whom Matthew is speaking and writing.

Many recognized the Messiah in Jesus just as many recognized Yahweh as their only Lord. The inclusion of the visit of the magi to the little newborn child and to his mother is set in this perspective. "They were overjoyed at seeing the star, and on entering the house, found the child with Mary his mother. They prostrated themselves and did him homage" (2:10–11a). For Matthew a new "epic" is beginning, one similar to that of the ancient Jewish people, now with new key figures, particularly Jesus and Mary.

Jesus, the central figure, is the new image of the faithful and persecuted people. Egypt reappears on the scene to recall the slavery of the people and their exodus. Now in the age of Roman domination, the context is different but the persecution of those who seek truth and justice is a constant, a sign in history that the establishment of the Kingdom of God is something that provokes fear and insecurity in the powers of this world. Hence, there are persecutions of various sorts.

The pilgrimage of Jesus, Mary, and Joseph recalls the pilgrimage of the people in fulfillment of the covenant: "After they had left, the angel of the Lord suddenly appeared in a dream to Joseph with the command: 'Get up, take the child and his mother, and flee to Egypt'" (Matt. 2:13). In Matthew's composition, the Old Testament is the background against which the new events are drawn. Hence, following the words of Hosea, "Out of Egypt I called my son" (Hos. 11:1), Joseph returns with Mary and the child to Galilee: "But after Herod's death, the angel of the Lord appeared in a dream to Joseph in Egypt with the command: 'Get up, take the child and his mother, and set out for the land of Israel. . . .' He got up, took the child and his mother, and returned to the land of Israel" (2:19–21).

It is from the land of Israel that God is going to show salvation once more. God takes on human flesh, new signs begin to occur: the blind see, lepers become clean, the dead arise. These are the signs of the Kingdom of God, signs of God's presence in our midst, signs that will lead to the crucifixion of Jesus, crucifixion of the faithful people:

> After the sabbath, as the first day of the week was dawning, Mary Magdalene came with the other Mary to inspect the tomb. Suddenly there was a mighty earthquake, as the angel of the Lord descended from heaven. He came to the stone, rolled it back, and sat on it. . . . Then the angel spoke, addressing the women: "Do not be frightened. I know you are looking for Jesus the crucified, but he is not here. He has been raised, exactly as he promised" (Matt. 28:1–2, 5–6).

The story of the faithful people continues despite the crucifixion, and this is announced to the women, as a promise of life,

as a sunny morning that can be expected despite the darkness
of the tomb.

> It is dark, but not so dark,
> It is dark but I am singing,
> For tomorrow will come . . . (Thiago de Mello).

Hope is continually reborn, the hope of a dawn full of life,
the hope of the history of all peoples; and the resurrection of
Jesus, the resurrection of humankind, continually fosters hope.
In this endless resurrection, Matthew's Mary is the symbol of
virgin hope, the woman pregnant with life, the countenance of
the people full of light, the countenance of God, ever reborn
out of the ruins of destruction.

(c) The Mother of the Rejected One: Mary in Mark

In the Gospel of Mark we find few traces of Mary's life. Our
first impression is that Mark is not interested in providing any
information on Mary because she does not seem very important.
His basic interest is to present Jesus living the paradox of his
mission. On the one hand he is sent and exalted by God and on
the other he is not understood and is rejected by the Jews and
even by his family. We find it disconcerting to think that Jesus'
blood relatives, including his mother Mary, should have an attitude like the one that seems quite clear in Mark 3:20–21: "He
returned to the house with them and again the crowd assembled,
making it impossible for them to get any food whatever. When
his family heard of this they came to take charge of him, saying,
'He is out of his mind.' "

All indications are that Mark wants to accentuate the extremes between the acceptance and rejection of Jesus, and so
we can speak of a clear theological intention, namely to point
out the scandal of a Messiah who is crucified despite the expressions of strength and power (cures, miracles, confrontations with
demons) shown throughout his life. We cannot conclude from
this that Mary, Jesus' mother, would have been opposed to her
son's basic enterprise, that is, to the the Kingdom of God as
described in the early prophetic tradition. We cannot believe

that Mary thought her son was really "out of his mind" and that
she was bewildered by his actions. To some extent that would
reinforce a *macho* vision of the weakness and limitations of
women when it comes to understanding crucial situations.

We believe Mark wants to emphasize an extreme, the extreme
of rejection, in order to make clear a basic theological affirmation in the following text (3:31–5) — Jesus' "true" family, or in
other words, the family made up of those who do God's will.
Blood ties are not spurned, but rather surpassed or set within
another perspective. There is a new communion and a new family community set up on the basis of activity for the sake of the
Kingdom. " 'Who are my mother and my brothers?' And gazing
around him at those seated in the circle he continued, 'These
are my mother and my brothers. Whoever does the will of God
is brother and sister and mother to me' " (3:33–5).

It is Mark's theological purpose to emphasize a new way for
persons to relate to one another, one whose starting point is
God. This new way of relating goes beyond social conventions
and apparent love, and it leads to splits and causes scandal, for
it is based on another way of living and bringing about justice
among persons.

Mark does not seem concerned about revealing how Jesus
feels toward Mary, or vice versa. He has no interest in answering
naive and curious questions about the filial or maternal relationship between the two. He does not write a pedagogical tract
on how Jesus might have rebelled against his family or about
how Mary might have taught him to rebel or might have "supported" his rebellion. Such speculations, which spring up in
many people's imaginations, do not concern the evangelist in
the least.

Another text in which Mark recalls Mary refers to the puz-
zlement that the actions and teachings of her son prompted in
Nazareth.

> He departed from there and returned to his own part of
> the country followed by his disciples. When the sabbath
> came he began to teach in the synagogue in a way that
> kept his large audience amazed. They said: "Where did he
> get all this? What kind of wisdom is he endowed with?

How is it that such miraculous deeds are accomplished by his hands? Is this not the carpenter, *the son of Mary,* a brother of James and Joseph and Judas and Simon? Are not his sisters our neighbors here?" They found him too much for them. Jesus' response to all this was: "No prophet is without honor except in his native place, among his own kindred, and in his own house" (6:1–4).

In this text as in the previous ones, Jesus is the center of Mark's concerns. Mary is mentioned in order to highlight the scandal produced by Jesus' actions. Is this not the son of Mary? After all, a carpenter, someone of no great social importance, a lowly man born in Nazareth, how could he speak and act as a Jew, yet in a way so different from the prevailing kind of Judaism? Nevertheless, it seems that from Nazareth, a tiny village that counts for nothing politically and economically, something new is being born, something that can produce tremors in the seats of power in Judaism at that time when legalism held sway and the poor were forgotten. The "innovator" from Nazareth is Mary's son. It seems that it is through her and his "brothers" that Jesus is identified. Here Jesus' sonship is tied to a woman, his mother, Mary. Mary's motherhood is a historical reference point, a fact that can identify the carpenter who works miracles, knows the law and the prophets, and defends the poor. That identity leads to astonishment and bewilderment. After all, "What kind of wisdom is he endowed with?" Again in a way specific to his theology, Mark brings out the extreme of the rejection of Jesus: not even in his own country and among his own is he acknowledged.

Despite the fact that Mark's central theological concern is with Jesus and with the mystery surrounding his person, it is significant that he says so little about Mary. We believe his silence is due not only to his central theological concern, but that it also reflects something real about Jewish society which was built and described in male-centered terms. This does not mean that women did not participate in building a community of equal disciples[22] and in announcing the Kingdom of God to the poor, since in various ways they appear in Mark's text as "benefitting" from a connection to Jesus — see, for example, the cure of a woman suffering a hemorrhage (5:25ff.) or the cure of the daughter of Jairus (5:41). A woman is the first witness and first messenger of the resurrection: "Jesus rose from the dead early on the first day of the week. He first appeared to Mary Magdalene, out of whom he had cast seven demons. She went to announce the good news to his followers, who were now mourning and weeping. But when they heard that he was alive and had been seen by her, they refused to believe it" (16:9–11).

They "refused to believe" in a woman's "delirium." After all she had had seven devils inside her and she was only a woman. Nevertheless, Mark emphasizes that she was the first person to whom Jesus appeared, as though to give a sure indication that women and men participated equally in the Jesus movement.

Mary, the mother of Jesus, is part of this milieu which both opens and closes space for women, a milieu of patriarchal tradition that insists that women be subject to men, as we have already noted. Nevertheless, we believe that in Mark's theology, which, as we have seen, highlights the extremes of "acceptance" and "rejection" of Jesus and the "scandal" of his person, Mary, his mother, is part of this theological intention and composition. On the one hand, Mary is set on the side of the humankind that "almost" rejects him and is involved with the very group of those who believe that he has gone "out of his mind." On the other hand, she is set forth as a figure who rises above the biological level of a relationship with Jesus and is among those who do God's will (see 3:35).

In Mary, Jesus is begotten by Mary's humanity, and this means that he is begotten under the sign of contradiction, conflict, division. Mary is the symbol of this humankind in which God's newness takes place and in which the poor have their turn because the announcing of the Kingdom starts with them.

(d) In Mary's Womb, God's Work in Human Flesh: A Poetic Moment in Luke

Luke is the evangelist who provides us with the greatest number of ingredients for a Marian theology. We could even say that in him we find both the good news of Jesus and the good news of Mary, deeply complementary and closely inter-related. Luke knows how to use the Old Testament brilliantly by turning it into a cloth on which "new events" are "embroidered" and on which a new and different light is cast.

The central idea of Luke's text, which reappears step-by-step throughout his writing and which is experienced in the different Christian communities with which he is familiar, is that *God has become human flesh.* This God is none other than Yahweh, the Lord, the Savior and Creator of God's people. In order to express this "newness" whose consequences are immense for Judaism and for the history of humankind, Luke retrieves the Old Testament in a very original fashion. It is not the property of the Jews but the inheritance of all those peoples who accept the active presence of the living God in history.[23]

Luke prepares a very beautiful theological composition and through it goes on to reveal "the events which have been fulfilled in our midst, precisely as those events were transmitted to us by the original eye-witnesses and ministers of the word" (1:1–2).

We are going to go through Luke's Gospel simply attempting to highlight those aspects that are relevant to a Marian theology, using some important texts. Therefore our reflection is limited to a specific objective.

The first text to consider describes the annunciation to Mary: 1:26–38. This text follows the religious and literary style of theophanies, which are manifestations of God in the life of the people. Mary is first of all the people receiving a "revelation" from God. Mary is the people in which this "revelation" is being effected. Luke's composition prepares the reader for the reception of a collective event, although the actors on stage are individual persons. Since the content of the announcement goes beyond the life of a few individuals, we can say that Mary is both an individual figure and symbol of the people awaiting the Messiah.

The reception of the "divine action" in history, the theologico-existential expression of the annunciation, is built on the prophecy of Isaiah. What the prophet announces is realized now with Mary and with Jesus.

Therefore the Lord himself will give you this sign: the virgin shall be with child, and bear a son, and shall name him Immanuel (Isa. 7:14).

The people who walked in darkness
have seen a great light;
Upon those who dwelt in the land of gloom
a light has shone (Isa. 9:1).

But a shoot shall sprout from the stump of Jesse,
and from his roots a bud shall blossom.
The spirit of the lord shall rest upon him:
a spirit of wisdom and of understanding,
a spirit of counsel and of strength,
a spirit of knowledge and of fear of the Lord.
(Isa. 11:1–2)

Therefore in Luke the Lord visits a virgin and begins to dwell in her. The Immanuel, or "God with us," is born of a virgin people, of a new people, not given over to idols, not sharing in injustice. The virgin is "betrothed to a man named Joseph, of the house of David." Hence the newness is connected to the hopes of the ancient Jewish people, and has to do with what the ancients hoped for but did not see. Now these hopes are being fulfilled in an open-ended way. The signs of the Kingdom are occurring, and God's kingship is manifest to some extent in continuity with Israel's hopes and yet also is breaking away from those hopes. It is in the people who are "little ones," the poor from all corners of the universe, that the signs of victory of life over death will appear. The Kingdom does not come with some grandiose event, like a victory at the end of a long battle, but it is breaking out here and there, wherever justice and love are becoming victorious in the great and small efforts of human existence, efforts that begin anew with each generation, as the days go on in the variety of places where human history unfolds.

It is this wonderful recognition that God is becoming event in our midst that leads Luke to make the angel greet Mary, "Hail, full of grace." The woman, bosom of the new people, dwelling of the Lord, is graced by the Lord's presence in a baby. Luke no doubt has Zephaniah in mind: "The King of Israel . . . is in your midst" (Zeph. 3:15b). "Shout for joy, O daughter Zion!, sing joyfully, O Israel!" (Zeph. 3:14).

What is announced to Mary forms part of the many manifestations of God's fidelity to God's people. We may recall the "annunciation" to Hagar,[24] Sarai's slave: "The Lord's messenger found her by a spring in the wilderness ... and he asked, 'Hagar maid of Sarai, where have you come from and where are you going? ... I will make your descendants so numerous.... You are now pregnant and shall bear a son; you shall name him Ishmael, for the Lord has heard you, God has answered you'" (Gen. 16:7–11). The annunciation to Abraham is in this same line:

> When Abram was ninety-nine years old, the Lord appeared to him and said, ... "Between you and me I will establish my covenant, and I will multiply you exceedingly.... My covenant with you is this: you are to become the father of a host of nations.... As for your wife Sarai, do not call her Sarai; her name shall be Sarah. I will bless her, and I will give you a son by her" (Gen. 17:1–22).

We may also recall the announcement of the birth of Samson: "An angel of the Lord appeared to the woman and said to her: 'Though you are barren and have had no children, you will conceive and bear a son'" (Judg. 13:2–25). In the New Testament the annunciation to Zachary is along the same lines (Luke 1:11–22).

A message from the Lord is always something extraordinary within the ordinariness of life, as though all such messages sought to remind us of the breakthrough of transcendence, of the wonderful, within the limits of our existence. "Annunciations" carry this dimension touching the root of the human, revealing its hidden possibilities, reviving its hope for life. "Annunciations" always have to do with life, the continuity of the people, the faithful presence of God in their midst.

In most details the angel's annunciation to Mary follows the same structure as other "annunciations," except that the one who is announced and is born is the "son of the Most High," and of him it is said that "his reign will be without end." Now it is no longer God giving a blessing so the people will be blessed with posterity as in the Old Testament, but rather what is announced to Mary is the "incarnation" of God in the midst of God's people. Now God will be found in the midst of the people, and what God wants will in fact be accomplished to the extent that a world of brothers and sisters is actually built up. Hence, theologically speaking, this "annunciation" is different. Here it is God who announces God's own coming. That is why Mary does not know man — "The Holy Spirit will come upon you and the power of the Most High will overshadow you; hence, the holy offspring to be born will be called Son of God" (Luke 1:35). This theological change in the style of annunciation reveals the historic appearance of a break with traditional Judaism. We can detect something different happening in Palestine at that *fin de siècle,* that moment of historic tensions under Roman domination.[25]

No "new belief" takes shape without preparation and historic causes that give rise to it. The recognition of Jesus as God's face in history is unquestionably the outgrowth of a very important process of cultural maturation. Faith in the incarnation signifies a true religious revolution, embodied in a special way in the first century of our era.

We need only recall the movement of John the Baptist in which Jesus seems to have taken part for a while. We see him being baptized by John, for example, a sure indication that he first belonged to the Baptist's group.

The evangelists witness the fact that there were disciples of John and disciples of Jesus, alongside other dissident movements within first-century Judaism (Zealots, Sadducees, Essenes, and so forth). This means that even before Jesus there were clear signs that something new was stirring within Judaism, in the direction of what was called the incarnation of the Word of God. That represents the gradual growth of a kind of "new schism" within an apparently homogeneous religion. A new understanding of God, taken on by the Jesus movement, rekindled the prophetic hope of a God vindicating the poor.

This all helps us to understand what is new in the announcement made to Mary. This woman, image of the faithful and servant people, answers, "I am the servant of the Lord. Let it be done to me as you say" (Luke 1:38). The expression "servant of the Lord" takes us back to 2 Samuel 7:5–11, where David, the servant of the Lord, wants to build the Lord a house. In different ways the Lord answers that that dwelling has always been in the midst of the people, like that of a "wayfarer." Mary-and-people constitute the new "Ark of the Covenant," God's dwelling, where God can be encountered and loved. Luke assimilates the experiences and theological expressions of the Jews and gives them a new meaning that grows out of the newness experienced by Jesus' followers.

The deep meaning of "Let it be done to me as you say" cannot be disconnected or isolated from the effect of the word of the Lord throughout the experience of the Old and New Testaments. The effect of the word of the Lord in Jewish-Christian religious experience can be summed up in the words of the prophet Isaiah:

> The spirit of the Lord God is upon me. . . .
> He has sent me to bring glad tidings to the lowly,
> to heal the brokenhearted,
> To proclaim liberty to the captives
> and release to the prisoners,
> To announce a year of favor from the Lord.
>
> (61:1–2)

It could also be summarized in the ancient prayer of the Magnificat that Luke puts on Mary's lips. This means that the word of the Lord is something concrete that has an impact in history, and it also means that the word of the Lord is not a call uncritically to accede to an outrageously unjust situation.

Over the centuries Mary's *fiat* or "Let it be done" has been interpreted in a highly subjectivist manner, almost like a conformist acceptance, which is then held up as a virtue — it is put forth as showing an exemplary religious and spiritual attitude, that of obedience to God. The sometimes exaggerated emphasis on the religious attitude of submission has obscured the aspect of a historic significance that goes beyond individuals. This has especially been the experience of women, for whom Mary's "yes" has been interpreted as an unconditional acceptance of the order laid down by men. In this way, Mary's acceptance has been used improperly. From the biblical and theological per-

spective we are presenting here, that acceptance stands in continuity with the creation of a new earth, of new relations between
men and women. In the final chapter of this essay we shall return
to the question of Mary's assent in the light of the Magnificat.

The second text to consider is that which depicts Mary's visit
to Elizabeth, known as the Visitation. Mary goes into Zechariah's house and greets Elizabeth. It is impossible to ignore the
fact that the site for the announcement to Zechariah is the
temple (Luke 1:8–22), which was extremely important in official
Judaism. The site for the announcement to Mary is her house.
However, Mary goes to Zechariah's house to be with Elizabeth
and serve her. So there is a significant shift from temple to
house. The house is a more familiar place, one closer to ordinary
people, and it indicates the shift from Judaism to Christianity.
The son of the priest is announced in the temple, while the son
of the woman Mary is announced at her house. Mary's visit to
Elizabeth signifies the encounter of the new with the old, and
it takes place in the home, the place for family intimacy. This
meeting is the sign of the acknowledgment of the new by the
old, at least on the part of the Jewish population. The old is the
ancient Jewish people, faithful to the traditions of Moses; the
new is what is present in Mary, what is being begotten in her
womb and what causes the baby to "leap" in Elizabeth's womb
and causes her to be "filled with the Holy Spirit" (1:41). "The
moment your greeting sounded in my ears, the baby leapt in my
womb for joy" (1:44). The ancient people swells with hope and
trembles with joy, for old age and sterility once more see life,
indeed a life conjoined with marvelous newness. Hence John is
called "prophet of the Most High; for you shall go before the
Lord to prepare straight paths for him" (Luke 1:76).

Elizabeth's dialogue with Mary ("Blest are you among women
and blest is the fruit of your womb. But who am I that the mother
of my Lord should come to me?" [Luke 1:42–43]) takes us back
to the book of Judith and to 2 Samuel 6. In Judith 13:18 we
read: "Then Uzziah said to her: 'Blessed are you, daughter, by
the Most High God, above all the women on earth.'" Just as
Judith is the figure of the woman/people giving birth to the
people's salvation, so also is Mary.

It is good to remind ourselves of the collective aspect of the woman figure and not take it just in its individual aspect, thereby falling into the error indicated in Chapter II, sections 2 and 3, that of losing sight of the real texture of history and of the way the activities of innumerable individuals are connected. Mary is now the one who is "blessed among women." The one who recognizes and proclaims that fact is Elizabeth, the old Jewish woman who gives birth to the last of the prophets of the Old Law. This meeting and dialogue between two women who are "graced" by God in different ways has a deep theological meaning. We believe Luke was not trying merely to exalt Mary's qualities of service and Elizabeth's qualities of hospitality and praise for her cousin, but to build up a theological text with a precise theological intention. In this theological intention, men and women are equally present as those who bring about the new event of the Kingdom of God. Elizabeth bears John in her womb and Mary bears Jesus. Both bear a history, a history of the Jewish people, one full of conflict, hope, despair, and yet always open to new hope. The two do not just happen to come together; in symbolic terms their meeting is the expression of something more than an event that someone retells much later. The event both expresses the recognition of the "new" by the "old," as we have previously stated, and in Mary's song it reveals that women fully participate in the prophetic mission of announcing and bringing about God's Kingdom.

Their "conversation" is about God's wonders because it is in them that these wonders take place. Hence they represent both women and the people as a whole, men and women. This is the collective expression of a people's faith masterfully presented in the story of the encounter between two women, both pregnant with life.

Second Samuel 6 deals with carrying the Ark of the Covenant to Jerusalem. The ark stayed in the house of Obed-edom the Gittite for three months, and then it was taken to the city of David. Everyone then rejoiced and "David came dancing before the Lord with abandon." Luke certainly went searching through the Old Testament for "these vessels of precious dye." He made use of them to speak of the new Ark of the Covenant made flesh, woven of flesh and recognized as what God has done through human flesh.

This central core, which in summary form we call incarnation, is the basis around which Luke's text is organized, and it is also the source of the new power that the old poem taken from the ancient traditions of the people and from the prophetesses of the Old Testament assumes on Mary's lips. "My being proclaims the greatness of the Lord,/my spirit finds joy in God my savior" (1:46). This is not the adolescent joy described in those old fables that told how Mary like other adolescents aspired to be the mother of the Savior. Mary's joy expresses the joy of the people that lives and proclaims the wonders of the presence of God who looks down on that people and brings about justice in the people's midst. This is why Mary gives voice to a synthesis of the joy and hope of the people in the past, present, and future:

> He has shown might with his arm. . . .
> He has deposed the mighty from their thrones
> and has raised the lowly to high places.
> The hungry he has given every good thing,
> while the rich he has sent empty away.
> He has upheld Israel his servant,
> ever mindful of his mercy;
> even as he promised our fathers. . . .
>
> (Luke 1:47–55)

There is no end to the Lord's help and promise. This is the experience underlying religious expressions like the Magnificat. Deep down there is an experience of the ever-renewed possibility of hope, the never-ending desire for justice, the ever-renewed yearning for a love that can satisfy the eternal yearning to love. "His mercy is from age to age: on those who fear him" (1:50). Each generation takes up again this ceaseless quest, and leaves as a legacy the insatiable yearnings for love, mercy, justice — yearnings that are limited expressions of what is called the love of God.

Mary's song is a war chant, God's battle song enmeshed in human history, the struggle to establish a world of egalitarian relationships, of deep respect for each individual, in whom godhead dwells. That is why there is mention of confounding the proud, of deposing the mighty, of sending the rich away empty-handed for the glory of God. It is from the mouth of a woman that this song of the battle against evil emerges, as though a new people could only be born from the womb of a woman. The image of the pregnant woman, able to give birth to the new, is the image of God who through the power of God's Spirit brings to birth men and women committed to justice, living out their relationship to God in a loving relationship with other human beings. Mary's song is the "program of the Kingdom of God," which is similar to Jesus' program which is read in the synagogue at Nazareth (4:16–21). Here the relationship between Mary and Jesus is not simply one of motherhood and childhood; both are signs and a living presence of the new people of God, of that people that overcomes the ties of flesh and becomes family in the Holy Spirit.

The third text from Luke's Gospel we will consider in an effort to find its meaning for us today is that which depicts Mary's delivery, usually known as the story of the birth of Jesus. Luke places Mary's delivery in a historical setting. It takes place under Roman domination, under the power of the emperor Caesar Augustus, during a census carried out by imperial edict. The delivery takes place in Bethlehem of Judea. It is there that Mary gives "birth to her first born son" (2:7).

Special circumstances surround her delivery. It takes place away from where she lives, on a journey undertaken to comply with an order from the established power. She apparently does not suffer great pains and it is said that she has to stay in a stable, since "there was no room for them in the place where travelers lodged" (2:7b). There is no mention of midwives or of any women from that place who might have come to help a woman whose "time was come." There is mention, however, of shepherds who are watching their flocks. After hearing the news from an "angel of the Lord," they come to see the mother and child. Mentioned also is a magnificent chorus of angels "praising God and saying, 'Glory to God in high heaven, peace on earth to those on whom his favor rests' "(2:14).

The picture Luke paints is a true theophany or manifestation of God to God's people. This manifestation takes place in the midst of the events of history, in the midst of its conflicts, in the midst of domination by a foreign political power. But God "is begotten" in the flesh of those who are faithful to the Spirit of the Lord, and Mary is the pre-eminent symbol of such fidelity. Those who recognize it are simple people, poor shepherds who are able to hear voices of angels and tremble at the event of life.

The visit of the shepherds and their haste recall the haste of Mary, Joseph, and the infant lying in the manger (2:16). Here it is no longer the ancient people recognizing the "newness" of Jesus, but the poor, those from whom practically nothing is expected. It is they who recognize in Jesus the new hope, the wonderful presence of God in the midst of human poverty.

Hence it can be said that Mary and the shepherds are like a coin: on one side the face of the woman and on the other the faces of the shepherds, the faithful people. One does not exist without the other. If we twirl the coin, the mass of faces blurs into the face of Mary. They become one face, a single people in motion giving birth to God's life in human history.

This is why it is important that we think about Mary's giving birth and that we think about the collective theological significance of this delivery, a delivery in which all of us, women and men, are involved in a way that goes beyond the bounds of human biology and physiology. This is the birth of God within humankind. That is why it is so magnificent in its simplicity and so extraordinarily mysterious. There is only one attitude possible when we stand before beauty and tremble with enchantment as we recognize a Presence: "Mary treasured all these things and reflected on them in her heart" (2:19). Posture of silence, of contemplation in the face of the ever greater mystery. Mystery in the woman, in the child, in the man, in the shepherds. Mystery of God's presence in the confines of the human.

This is not a passive attitude on the part of the woman Mary toward these events, as though she were simply accepting what she did not understand in the least. In Mary we experience silence in the presence of the God who is greater than we, in the presence of God's presence and transcendence in women, in men, in the child. Mary's presence cannot be isolated from the presence of the faithful people, just as Jesus cannot be isolated from the people to whom he is sent. Luke puts his text together by utilizing individuals who have a collective aspect that extends to the Christian community of his time and to us today.

In his Gospel Luke alludes directly to Mary in two more texts. One is the presentation in the temple where the old man Simeon speaks to her in these words: "This child is destined to be the downfall and the rise of many in Israel, a sign that will be opposed—and you yourself shall be pierced with a sword—so that the thoughts of many hearts may be laid bare" (2:34–5).

The second text speaks of Jesus in the temple among the teachers of the law and of the anxiety of Mary and Joseph as they search for him. "When his parents saw him they were astonished, and his mother said to him: 'Son, why have you done this to us? You see that your father and I have been searching for you in sorrow'" (Luke 2:48).

Simeon's prophecy continues to be fulfilled today in our midst. Those who struggle for the Kingdom of God are marked by contradiction in relation to this world. A sword keeps running through the hearts of the poor and of those who struggle for God's justice, for men and women throughout the world know that until the end we must be primarily "occupied with the things" of God's Spirit. Anyone who is concerned about them and commits his or her life to them is singled out for persecution and at the same time is seized with the passion of those who from generation to generation want to save the world.

(e) Mary in the Events of the Early Church: The Acts of the Apostles

Mary's name is mentioned only once in the Acts of the Apostles: "Together they devoted themselves to constant prayer. There were some women in their company, and Mary the mother of Jesus and his brothers"(1:14).[26] In addition, Acts hints at her presence on the day of Pentecost, symbol of the New Creation in the Spirit of God. All exegetes take it for granted that she was present. All those present were united and were filled with the Spirit; like Mary, Elizabeth, Jesus, and Stephen, all were filled with the Spirit in order to go on announcing and experiencing God's wonderful deeds.

We believe it is not accidental that in the Acts of the Apostles Luke, the evangelist who says most about Mary in his Gospel, recalls her at these moments and only these moments. Luke's text leads us to recognize that after Jesus' death, Mary and the other women remained closely connected to Jesus' closest disciples, to the twelve apostles and probably to others, men and women, not mentioned in the text. There are indeed clear indications that there was a community formed in the spirit of the Jesus who "did and taught from the beginning until the day he was taken up to heaven by the Holy Spirit" (1:1–2).

However, such a reading tells us little about Mary. We simply know that she was there with those who carried on Jesus' mission. We should like to discover something more, to know just how she acted in an early Christian community, to know more about how she proclaimed the Kingdom, what problems she experienced, and how her days as a "servant of the Lord" ended.

The New Testament does not satisfy our hunger for such answers, and the text of Acts even less so. Nevertheless we believe we must pursue the few flashes we have in order to see what we can discern beyond the little we can see by reading the text with the unaided eye.

The book of Acts begins with the ascension, that is, when Jesus is definitively withdrawn and from which point his activity is to be continued through his disciples. Mary was part of this continuity even though that is not stated specifically. She participated in the church in Jerusalem and no doubt experienced the most decisive events that contributed to its being built up. She undoubtedly experienced the anguish of the persecution by Jews and Romans which Christians at that time suffered, as the Acts of the Apostles and historic documents from that period describe.

She also experienced Pentecost, the awareness of the presence of the Spirit in the community that proclaimed the good news of the Kingdom. The backdrop for the text that narrates Pentecost is the Old Testament and especially Exodus 19:16ff. The text about Pentecost depicts a theophany, a new manifestation of the Lord, the same Lord who from the beginning created everything that exists and whose self-manifestation to the ancient Jewish people has occurred in various ways. Now this same God sends God's Spirit to all "peoples, races and nations."

There is a veritable explosion of Christian awareness, going beyond the Jewish movement that Jesus began, an explosion that recognizes that God's greatness is no longer limited to a single nation but is present in all human flesh, temple of God's love. It is a new creation, a new perception of God's presence which begins in a particular group, but is aimed at the whole of humankind.

Mary is present at this explosion, in this great innovating movement. We could not imagine it in any other way even if the texts written at that time speak essentially about movements and groups led by men.

Luke is quite "discreet" about Mary's presence, but we have a right to use our creative historic imagination to go beyond what is said, to rescue the forgotten memory in order to recall the presence of the one who in the early tradition, and especially the tradition subsequent to the first-century Christian communities, has occupied a position of fundamental importance in the lives of all Christians. The numerous devotions to Mary in the East and later in the West attest to this point. Hence it can be said that Mary was at the core of the foundation of the early Christian communities as the mother, sister, colleague, disciple, and teacher of a movement organized by her son Jesus. At the core of the historic roots of that movement is the announcement that the Kingdom of God is present in the midst of the poor, those whom established power does not recognize at all.

By recovering or "reconstructing" creatively the data, we make Mary once more a participant in the concrete story of the early communities and we restore to history the truth about the activity of Mary and the other women.[27] We also force Christian communities today to acknowledge the real participation of men and women, and especially Mary, in the struggle for the Kingdom of God in the history of former times. That vision leads us to overcome the limitations of the texts and historic documents which, due to their unavoidably selective perspective, fail to tell us much about women. It also situates us in a more realistic vision of history, which is built by men and women, who, although they carry out different tasks, are both builders of life in society. Hence in the early Christian community in Jerusalem, "all," "with some women, including Mary," "preached God's wonderful works."[28]

(f) Mary — Present in the Time of Signs and at the "Hour" of Jesus: The Gospel of John

In the fourth Gospel, we find two passages that refer explicitly to Mary. Although these two episodes are quite far apart in the context of the narratives, nevertheless they can be interpreted as though they were closely related and mutually attracting one another.[29]

The first is that of the wedding at Cana (2:1–12), placed in a wedding banquet which Mary attends, as do Jesus and his disciples (vv. 1–2). The geographical location is important: Cana of Galilee[30] was looked down on at that time in Palestine, for "no prophet would come" from there (7:52). Contrary to that attitude, the evangelist sets the first manifestation of the prophet par excellence, Jesus of Nazareth, in this poor region, in this small town; thus the setting runs contrary to the expectations of the Pharisees and other powerful ones at that time.

Similarly, the time in which the evangelist sets the account is filled with significance: "On the third day there was a wedding at Cana in Galilee . . ." (2:1). Such seemingly chronological precision immediately alerts the reader of the Gospel to a *kairos* — a qualitatively different time when God's eternity invades human history. In biblical terms, *the third day* — when the sign at Cana takes place — is related to the event of Sinai in the book of Exodus and to the resurrection.

Arriving at Sinai under Moses' leadership, the people encountered the expected revelation of Yahweh's glory made concrete in the handing down of the law, all of which took place "on the third day." The people then accepted their election and believed in their God thus made manifest to them (Exod. 19:9–11). It was also on the third day that Jesus revealed his glory and his disciples believed the words he had said about his rising from the dead (see John 2:19–21). As set here the Cana episode reworks the great event of Sinai, now in the new light of the very incarnation of God made new law in the time and history of humankind. A prefiguration of the paschal era, which will become fully manifest in the resurrection, the sign performed at Cana takes place in the context of a wedding feast, in which the covenant of God with humankind begun at Sinai and definitively confirmed at the Pasch is celebrated. The water of the ancient Jewish purification rituals gives way to the new wine, better and more abundant (v. 10), a sign of the new people which receives the new law, the fullness of God's gift, which is superior to the law of Moses.

In the midst of this wedding celebration Mary is once more a figure of the people. She is the faithful people yearning and hoping for the messianic times so often promised. In the statement the evangelist places on her lips, "They have no more wine" (v. 3), we can read the deep desire the people feel for their own liberation: the old Mosaic institutions are no longer sufficient. The old wine runs out. And Mary—figure of the people recognizing this fact—hopes, desires, and acts so that the messianic times, so ardently yearned for, may arrive.

Jesus' response to Mary identifies her as woman: "Woman, how does this concern of yours involve me? My hour has not yet come" (v. 4). Attempting once more to read this pericope within the Bible as a whole, we see that Mary is here again confirmed as a figure of the people. In the Bible, the woman often represents the people (Ezek. 16:8; 23:2–4; Jer. 2:2; Hos. 1–3; Isa. 26:17–18). By placing the term "woman" on Jesus' lips when he addresses his mother, the evangelist reinforces the possibility of seeing in her the personification of the faithful remnant of Israel on the threshold of messianic redemption.

Just as the gift of the ancient Mosaic law on Sinai went hand-in-hand with the people's adherence to Yahweh in faith, so also Mary, figure of the new messianic people, is persistent in her faith that the sign will be performed despite Jesus' statement that his time has not yet come (v. 4). The way she advises the servants, "Do whatever he tells you" (v. 5), recalls the words of the chosen people at Sinai: "Everything the Lord has said, we will do" (Exod. 19:8; 24:3, 7).

From that point onward, the Gospel describes the beauty of the unfolding of salvation in the midst of the history of the people. The faithful people, of which Mary is the figure, sees its hopes culminate in the fullness of God's gift, which joyfully pours out plenty of new wine, which is even better than the earlier one. The groom and bride holding the feast give way to Jesus and Mary, to the man and woman, the new leading figures in the boundless messianic banquet God offers God's people.

This first sign—*archē,* beginning and origin of the revelation of Jesus—contains the archetype of the other signs that will be done in order to announce that the Kingdom has arrived and is "already in your midst." Mary's faith begets and gives birth to the faith of the new messianic community: "Thus did he reveal his glory, and his disciples believed in him" (v. 11). It also initiates the time of the new people, the community of the Kingdom, in which poor and despised Cana of Galilee becomes the place where God's glory is made manifest, where men and women drink wine, make merry, and celebrate the wedding feast of their liberation.

The second episode is set at the core of the Passion, shortly before Jesus' death. The evangelist says that "near the cross of Jesus there stood his mother"—and other women. There are various points of connection with the Cana episode:

—Mary is there but she is not called by her name. Instead, she is referred to as the "Mother of Jesus" and she is addressed as *woman* (pointing back to Eve, mother of the living).

—Jesus' hour, not yet arrived at Cana, now arrives on the cross when Jesus goes from this world to the Father.

—The messianic sign performed at Cana is now approaching its fulfillment. After Jesus' words to his mother and to the beloved disciple, 19:28 reads: "After that, Jesus, realizing that everything was now finished . . . to fulfill the scripture . . ."[31]

All this underscores the importance of this account. The tone the evangelist gives to Jesus' words in verses 26 and 27 is another confirmation. "Seeing his mother there with the disciple whom he loved, Jesus said to his mother, 'Woman, there is your son.' In turn he said to the disciple, 'There is your mother.' From that hour onward, the disciple took her into his care."

These verses belong to a literary genre that exegetes call a "revelation pattern." The author of the fourth Gospel follows a literary model known to prophetic literature, which is used when the Lord wants to communicate a very important "revelation" by way of his spokespersons. The evangelist reworks this pattern under his own inspiration. Full of the same Holy Spirit that inspired the prophets, Jesus, the prophet of the Father par excellence, *sees* the woman and the disciple and *says* to each of them, "*There is* your son. . . . *There is* your mother." With these deeds and words, the evangelist seeks to place in Jesus' mouth an important revelation from God.

The dying one first addresses Mary, calling her "woman" (as at Cana and as elsewhere in the fourth Gospel, where he address the Samaritan woman [4:21], the adulterous woman [8:10], and Mary Magdalene [20:15]). Thus the term with which her Son addresses Mary at the moment of his death has deep resonances in the community. The early church understood Jesus' death as what would "gather into one all the dispersed children of God" (see 11:51–2).[32] In Judaism the dispersion of the children of God among the pagans wiped out all their identity and made them a non-people. In Johannine theology, these dispersed people are all the marginalized and the victims of all kinds of oppression (due to injustice, sin, illness) who will be reunited through the salvation brought by Jesus in the new community of the Kingdom.

In the Old Testament, Jerusalem, often represented as a woman, was the seat, the land of blessing, the secure gate, the holy city for which all the dispersed of Israel yearned; likewise Mary is now the New Jerusalem, the woman, the mother who will reunite all the deported and lost of Zion in the new temple which is the body of her dead and risen Son.

If the prophet said to the old Jerusalem, "Behold your children reunited together," now Jesus says to his mother: "Woman, behold your son" (John 19:26). A figure of the Israel that gives birth to the new people, of the Jerusalem that brings the dispersed together in its temple, Mary is the one who gives birth to the Christian community, the people of the new covenant, symbolized in the beloved disciple, who is everyone who receives and loves Jesus.[33]

Following the great female and maternal figures of the Old Testament, Deborah and the mother of the Maccabees, described as Israel's true mothers and guides, Mary appears as mother of the new community of men and women who are to become followers of Jesus because they will believe in the glory

of God manifested in him. Traditional Christian piety very early
interpreted this gospel text in the sense of seeing in Mary the
mother of Christians, the mother of the church. The full depth
of this *sensus fidelium* tells us that the gospel of the Passion puts
Mary at the center of the event of salvation, brought by Jesus
Christ, as a symbol of the people that will accept the message
of the Kingdom and the fullness of the messianic age.

(g) The Woman Clothed with the Sun Who Defeats the Dragon: Revelation

Chapter 12 of the final and latest book of the Bible — the book
of Revelation, or the Apocalypse, as we often call it — describes
a woman. Can we say that there is any reference to Mary in this
symbolism and in the intention of the seer who piles vision upon
vision before the eyes of our faith?

The seer of Revelation has in mind a woman in mourning
who along with her offspring is standing face-to-face with her
enemy, the dragon. Verse 9 describes this dragon as identical to
the ancient serpent, which refers back to Genesis 3:15, to the
creation account and the words addressed to the serpent, "I will
put enmity between you and the woman, and between your offspring and hers; he will strike at your head, while you strike at
his heel." In Revelation 12 this enmity of which Genesis speaks
is clearly present, depicted as a struggle between the dragon and
the woman and her offspring, identified in both a personal and
a collective sense: the male son is the Messiah king, but he is
also the people, the community of Israel on the way toward
messianic redemption.

The way the woman is depicted in Revelation 12:1–2 is overflowing with rich symbolism: "A great sign appeared in the
sky, a woman clothed with the sun, with the moon under her
feet, and on her head a crown of twelve stars. Because she was
with child she wailed aloud in pain as she labored to give birth."

To begin with, we see woman appear once more as a figure
of the people. She is a figure not only of the old people, which
sighs toward the Jerusalem that will bring it together, which
begets from its race the Messiah and believers, but also of the
new chosen people which has seen the glory of Yahweh, mani-

fested in the Messiah Jesus. Here the woman appears as the Ark of the Covenant, which is mentioned just before the passage we are examining (see Rev. 11:19).

The woman appears as a *sign,* a revelation offered by God. And she appears *"clothed* with the *sun."* She is dressed so as to signify the love and passionate tenderness of God who dresses the lilies of the field more wonderfully than King Solomon (see Matt. 6:30), who adorns God's spouse Israel with the finest garments and precious jewels (Ezek. 16:10–13a), and who bestows bounty on Zion (Isa. 52:1). God dresses this sign-woman with the sun, with all the light of God's own glory and power.

Under the woman's feet is the moon, the heavenly body which according to the biblical mind governs chronological time and its division into days, months, years, seasons.[34] Even while living in time, the woman-people of God is not subject to it and conditioned by it, since the covenant with God, although it is made in history, goes beyond merely chronological time.

On the woman's head is a crown of twelve stars, a crown of triumph and victory, a crown of light, which in Jewish thought is a mark of the just who will reach their glorification in heaven.[35] The number twelve refers to the twelve tribes, to the ancient people of Israel. Jesus made the twelve apostles judges of that people (see Matt. 19:28). Here on the woman's head the twelve stars encompass the twelve tribes of the old covenant, while they also expand forward toward the historic and eschatological reality of the new people of the new covenant, since the son who is born of her womb is the one who will bring together all nations and will be raised up close to God's throne (v. 5). His posterity is made up of "those who keep God's commandments and give witness to Jesus" (v. 17). The woman is she who at the end of the book will assume the form of the "bride of the lamb" and the "new Jerusalem" (21:2, 9).

In the figure of the woman in chapter 12 there is a confluence of the peoples of God of the old and the new alliance, which the seer places "in heaven" where she appears as a sign (v. 1) and on earth where she engages in battle with the dragon. The eschatological and the historic, the Old Testament and the New Testament come together in this shining woman, sign of God's people.

In contrast to her luminescent and triumphal aspect is the dramatic and sorrowful way she appears. Verse 2 describes her as "with child" and wailing "aloud in pain as she labored to give birth." Commonly used in the Bible to describe the tribulations surrounding the time of God's manifestation, the messianic era, the day of Yahweh, woman's birth pangs here point to the paschal mystery. The male child who comes from her womb in pain and who is to rule all the nations with a rod of iron echoes the description of the Davidic King in Psalm 2 in which the early community saw the figure of the Messiah. The fact that this same description is used again here and is applied to the Word of God in Revelation 19:15 guarantees that this Christological interpretation is legitimate.[36] The clash between the son and the dragon who wants to devour him (v. 4) and his being lifted up to God's throne (v. 5b) direct us to the central mystery of the death and resurrection of Jesus, here understood as a new birth that initiates the new time in which the dragon is defeated.

In this paschal context the woman-people of God, who suffers birth pangs and flees to the desert, is a figure of the persecuted church which experiences in its own body the tribulations of the Servant of Yahweh. However, it suffers in the hope that the Kingdom will be stronger than the forces of the anti-Kingdom and that the birth pangs will be followed by joy at the arrival of a strong, healthy, lively child. These feelings on the part of the persecuted and witnessing church recall the words the fourth Gospel places on Jesus' lips just before his "hour." To his shocked and afflicted disciples he promises the afflictions and anguish of a woman in labor who later does not even think about the difficulties she has experienced, so happy is she that a new child has been given to the world (see John 16:21–2).

In the desert to which she flees the woman is put to the test, but she does not hesitate in her hope for she knows that she enjoys God's protection and support (vv. 6–14). The forces of the anti-Kingdom do not have much time left (v. 12), for the desert is the intermediate step that comes before arriving in the promised land. The woman is called to victory, to be bride of the Lamb, the new Jerusalem where all those who observe God's commandments and hold on to the witness of Jesus (Rev. 21) will ultimately be united. Therefore the most direct way possible to interpret the woman of Revelation 12 is as the persecuted and martyred people of God that bears within itself Jesus' pledge of victory.

What possibilities might this interpretation open up for a Marian theology? The first interpretation of this sort took place in the fourth century and may have coincided with a developing Marian interest within the Christian community of the post-apostolic generations. It may also be that when Revelation was placed in the canon of scripture along with the Gospels of Luke and John, the various images of the Virgin (Luke 1–2), of the woman by the cross (John 19:15–17), and the woman giving birth to the Messiah (Rev. 12) might have reinforced one another.[37]

Even though, exegetically speaking, we are proceeding over terrain where there is little certainty, we nevertheless ponder over this figure of the woman in Revelation 12 with all our yearning today, striving, with the legitimacy we have as children of God and the respect that all theology must have toward the word of God, to detect the Mariological signs contained here.

The woman's painful labor and the fact that the male child is seized and taken up before God open the way to a Marian theological interpretation on the basis of the paschal mystery. The scene described in Revelation 12:4–5 can be read in light of John 16:21–3, where the passion and resurrection of Jesus are depicted in terms of the sorrow and joy of the birth process; and that same scene in Revelation can also be read in light of John 19:25–7, where the emphasis is on extension of the community of faithful followers of Jesus. What John describes in a historico-interpretative fashion, Revelation describes in terms of a symbolic vision. Let us now explore the implications of reading the passage in Revelation in these various lights.

In Jesus' "hour," at the moment of his delivery to the Father, the messianic community at the foot of the cross is represented by the beloved disciple and some women, among whom the evangelist singles out Jesus' mother. Through the words he addresses to her, Jesus extends Mary's motherhood to the community that will believe in him and follow him. In labor pangs, the woman clothed with the sun and crowned with stars in Revelation 12 represents the suffering of the faithful remnant of the chosen people at the moment when the Messiah, through the suffering of his passion, is "delivered" toward the glory of resurrection. The woman who has borne the male child, the Messiah king, also has her motherhood extended by the author of Revelation to "those who keep God's commandments and give witness to Jesus," who are called "the rest of her offspring" (v. 17). The old and new Israel are united in the person of the woman, set at the center of the paschal mystery. The woman draws us toward the person of Mary described in John 19:25–7; and thus this woman in Revelation 12 makes us think more of the image of the church that is sketched in those same verses in John's Gospel.

In labor pains the woman also expresses the early community's difficult way to faith which involved accepting a suffering Messiah. She also expresses the path traced by the first disciples of Jesus Christ in understanding the meaning of the persecutions and sufferings they underwent. According to Luke's testimony, Mary lived within the Jerusalem community and participated in it (Acts 1:14), a community that had very direct experience of persecution by Jewish authorities and the liberating power of God manifested in the resurrection.[38]

Thus, according to Revelation 12, Mary is the figure of the humble and hardworking faith of the people who suffer and believe in the crucified savior, without losing hope. She is also the figure of a church persecuted by the world, by the forces of the anti-Kingdom and by the powerful and oppressors of all kinds, who, like the dragon described in Revelation, want to "devour" her children and offspring, want to devour the projection of the Kingdom, anything that means life and freedom for the people, anything that is the mature fruit of the fruitful womb of the woman. Finally, she is also a figure of victorious humankind which actually has God, born of woman, as part of its own race and has in the resurrection God's pledge and guarantee.

The new people of God, of which Mary is symbol and figure, is the "*sign*" that appears for us today, in heaven and on earth. It is a sign that to the offspring of the woman-Eve (Gen. 3:15) — that is, to every human being — there have been given the grace and the power to triumph over the serpent; that grace and power have been given through the offspring of the woman-Mary, out of whose flesh the Spirit shaped God's incarnation. Through the womb of the woman-people of God have emerged salvation and the community of those "who keep God's commandments and give witness to Jesus."

CHAPTER IV

Marian Dogmas: Their New Meaning Arising from the Poor and the "Spirit" of Our Age

We now arrive at a point in our reflection that is both fascinating and sensitive: the meeting point between scripture and the life journey of the church that we call tradition. It is also the point where in the poverty of human words and in the midst of the need to respond to the longings of God's people, the church seeks formulas to state and make explicit basic aspects of the mystery of Mary. We are referring to the Marian dogmas, a matter that is ecumenically sensitive,[1] morally problematic,[2] and theologically challenging. Since this is not an area of theology in which everything is clear, theologians need to pay extra attention not only to the most arcane meanderings of the word of God but also to the most contemporary nuances of the circumstantial context in which they live.

Therefore before taking up each of the dogmas themselves, seeking to re-read them from within our Latin American context, and seeking to grasp what they have to tell us at this time when we see the church being born in the midst of the poor, let us try to situate ourselves in relation to the very idea of dogma. What is a dogmatic definition all about? How can we explain and delimit clearly what dogma means in the overall life of the church? How can a definition elaborated some centuries ago still have something to say to people today? We are venturing out into a tricky area with the humility and love for the truth that ought to characterize any work in theology.

The concept of dogma as understood today in the Catholic Church was settled relatively recently. Its more remote origins should be sought in the post-Tridentine controversy with Protestants, in the effort to limit polemics to what both sides regarded as having official value. However, matters were actually fixed by church authority later at Vatican Council I (1870), which stated that "all those things are to be believed with divine and Catholic faith which are contained in the word of God, written or handed down, and which the Church, either by a solemn judgement, or by her ordinary and universal magisterium, proposes for belief as having been divinely revealed" (DS 3011, TCC 91).

Hence as the council saw it, two elements constitute dogma: (1) its content: it must be a truth contained in revelation; and (2) its form: it must be a truth that the church has formulated and expressly proposed as an object of faith. The historic context that gave rise to this definition is quite illuminating: the aim was to safeguard the continuity of the preaching of the post-Tridentine church with that of the early church and to combat the "semi-rationalist" mentality that was threatening to subordinate the transcendence of faith to the sway of human reason. Hence the stance taken by the magisterium at Vatican I in laying out the claims of dogma was strictly one of *defending* the faith.

The subsequent radicalization of this conciliar posture degenerated into an impoverishment of Catholic teaching on faith as the juridical aspect was accentuated, thus reducing dogmas primarily to "dogmatic propositions that the faithful are obliged to accept under pain of formal heresy." This juridical emphasis was followed by a growing rigidity of the statements and formulas themselves, to the point where today in the general theological and cultural mindset, dogma may have the connotation of controversy, in the sense that it remains on the level of formal definitions and hence may impede the church's dialogue with the modern world and with other faiths.

It is our intention here, in re-reading the Marian dogmas, to rehabilitate the word "dogma" by retrieving and keeping in mind its true meaning. So we will now point out some landmarks for understanding what we mean by dogma.

The most remote origins of dogma must be sought not in the last century but in the early church, when because of the conflict between Judaizers and non-Judaizers the apostolic community convoked the First Council of Jerusalem and conveyed the position it adopted to other churches, saying: "It is the decision of the Holy Spirit, and ours too . . ." (Acts 15:28). The original Greek text uses the word *edoxen,* from which the word "dogma" derives. Thus, for the early church dogma was the decision "of the Holy Spirit, and ours too" (that of the apostles in charge of the community) to assure the unity of faith of the community, in the service of the saving truth of the gospel. The import of these references is that dogma should not succumb to the risk of rigidity, and fidelity to dogma should not become dogmatism.

In fidelity to these most remote origins, dogma, as it is formulated, must remain open; while remaining faithful to its original content, it must respond to the yearnings and questions of God's people. Its reference-point is not simply a juridical formula but the very Christian mystery itself, which is not a "logical mystery" but a "mystery of salvation." Moreover, dogma moves along with changing times and new needs in society and the church, seeking to point them toward the mystery of transcendence which is the heart of the church itself. One can therefore speak of an evolution of dogma paralleled by a deepening of the Christian mystery. What is permanent in dogma is its deepest foundation, the original mystery out of which it emerges.

With regard to the mystery to which we will now direct our attentive and loving gaze — the mystery of Mary — we intend to be guided by the idea of dogma just presented, remaining faithful to what has been said about this mystery, starting from the deposit of revelation throughout the past ages and continuing up to that given to men and women of our time and place: the myriad of the poor and oppressed who today in Latin America are striving to forge their own history and to find in the gospel the motivation for their liberation struggle. How can the Marian dogmas be re-read within this context in history and in the church? How can the Marian theology contained in history and in the church have a word to say in the process of liberation in which the people of Latin America are engaged?

Before reflecting more extensively about each one of these dogmas, we must lay down some assumptions in order to prepare the way.

1. SOME ASSUMPTIONS FOR RE-READING

First, an *anthropological assumption*. We are going to try to read these dogmas in fidelity to the anthropology guiding this outline of Marian theology, an anthropology explained in Chapter I. This anthropology seeks to take into account the recent progress of human and social sciences, which are attempting to overcome the anthropological vices that have most characterized and distorted the West. Among these we have singled out male-centrism, dualism, idealism, and one-dimensionalism, and we are making every effort to do our Marian theology, with its re-reading of dogmas, on the basis of an anthropology that is human-centered, unifying, realist, and pluri-dimensional. We are aware of the difficulty inherent in such an effort, since many of these dogmas were proclaimed during periods of history that had other anthropological visions. Nevertheless, we regard as worthwhile the theological effort to go beyond debilitated and out-of-date formulations and expressions in order to rescue the very heart of the mystery that continues to make dogma valid within the church.

Second, the *properly theological assumption*. Since we began our theological effort by making the idea of the Kingdom of God the unifying factor of Christian theology in its various aspects, and examined our biblical texts from that standpoint, we intend to remain faithful to that central assumption, now with regard to tradition and dogma. In re-reading the Marian dogmas that the church has proclaimed throughout so many centuries of Christianity, it will be our ongoing challenge to recognize the potential of these dogmas for announcing the coming of the

Kingdom of God; we shall also seek to discern the signs contained in those dogmas that can help set the Kingdom in motion.

Third, the *feminist assumption*. Talking about Mary means talking about woman — specifically a woman who was born and lived in Palestine two thousand years ago. Christian faith venerates the mystery of *this* particular woman and theology reflects on that mystery. Devotion to the one whom Christian faith calls "Our Lady" basically resides and is expressed in the theological facts proclaimed by Marian dogmas: Mary was Mother of God, Virgin, immaculate, and was assumed into heaven. The people of God preserves the memory of these facts in its devotion. Marian theology strives to reflect on the common thread running through and connecting these facts and giving them their substance. The mystery of Mary leads back to the greater mystery, the mystery of God, and it opens a unique and original perspective for viewing this mystery: the feminist perspective. The tradition of faith has concentrated on the feminine in Mary, the mother of Jesus. It has viewed all women's potentialities as realized in her. She is Our Lady because she is virgin, mother, wife, companion, widow, queen, wisdom, tabernacle of God, and so forth.[3] Moreover the very fact that it is two women who are here pondering this mystery, trying to develop it, opens up space and possibilities in this reflection, not for the traditional perspective already mentioned but for the kind we advocated in Chapter II of this work. To recognize in Marian dogmas the traces of the feminine as revealed by God, the theological face of the feminine element of God, God's face as seen from a feminist perspective, is something that we will be constantly striving to keep in mind here.[4]

Finally the *pastoral assumption*. At first glance, Marian dogmas look like statements characterized by theological inflation and doxological enthusiasm. In them the Marian mystery contemplated in the light of God's plan and paschal glory is exalted. Nevertheless, we cannot forget that this mystery is just as much a mystery of poverty and anonymity. The exaltation that understandably comes out in dogma cannot slide toward the mythological and hide what is essential in God's salvation, that is, making God's glory shine on what is regarded as insignificant, degrading, or marginal.[5] Marian dogmas, which exalt Mary, immaculately conceived, assumed into heaven, virgin and mother, must reflect a knowledge that in exalting her, they exalt precisely her poverty, her dispossession, and her simplicity. This is the only key for understanding the mystery of God's incarnation in human history, of which Jesus and Mary are the protagonists. This is, moreover, the only key for understanding the mystery of the church as community of salvation, holy and sinful, striving amidst the most diverse kinds of limitations and problems to be a sign of the Kingdom in the midst of the world. Further, this is the only condition that will enable the church, which sees the symbol or figure of itself in Mary, to be in Latin America today the church of the poor, those whom Mary declared liberated, fed, and exalted in the song of the Magnificat.

Finally, before proceeding to reflect on each dogma we must recall that there is a history leading up to the formulation and proclamation of every dogma. The historical, political, social, and cultural context of the moment of proclamation is very significant, for when the circumstances in which it was proclaimed are explained, the content of the proclamation itself is also clarified.

2. THE MYSTERY OF MARY, THE MOTHER OF GOD: THE *THEOTOKOS*

The first dogma on which we will reflect is that of Mary's divine motherhood since it is the oldest of those that the church has officially proclaimed.[6] The Greek term that sums up the mystery of faith contained in the dogma — *Theotokos,* Mother of God — appeared first in the Provincial Council of Alexandria, a preparatory Council for Nicea (318–20), but was officially proclaimed at the Council of Ephesus in 431. However, we can find the development of the Marian theology of the divine motherhood running through the three great councils of antiquity: Constantinople I (381), Ephesus, and Chalcedon (451). In our own time, Vatican II (1962–5) has taken up the teaching of these councils and shed new light on it.

Contrary to the case with other dogmas, whose biblical roots are challenged and which constitute genuine problems for ecumenism, Mary's divine motherhood has deep and solid scriptural references. Mary is most often referred to as mother in the New Testament (twenty-five times) while there are only two texts that refer to her as virgin—Luke 1:27 and Matthew 1:23. For the gospel narratives Mary is basically the *mother of Jesus.*

Paul's very early text, which we have previously considered (Gal. 4:4),[7] already speaks of the Son sent by the Father in the fullness of time, born of woman. Jesus there appears as pre-existing Son—"Son of the Father." By referring to Jesus as "Son of the Father," Paul makes it clear that Jesus of Nazareth is not merely a man who is especially good and cherished by God, something like a favorite son. Nor is he talking about someone who begins to exist in an absolute sense at the moment of the incarnation. It is none other than God—the Son, who shares the Father's divinity—whom the Father sends in the fullness of time and raises from the dead with the power of the Holy Spirit (see Rom. 1:1–4). It is God who takes human flesh.

The Son of the Father, who pre-exists from all eternity, and who has given us too the power to be children of God and call on this God as Father, is also just as much the "son of Mary" (see Mark 6:3; Matt. 13:55; John 6:42), "born of woman" (Gal. 4:4). Hence Mary's son is none other than God, who out of God's glory takes on the frailty and poverty of the human condition, among those "born of woman" (see John 15:14; 25:4). This is the descending kenotic process of incarnation which the letter to the Philippians exalts (2:5–8). Therefore it is none other than God who takes flesh in Mary's flesh and who having emerged in birth from her womb will shock his contemporaries, who upon seeing the wonders and powerful signs he performs will ask, "Isn't this the carpenter's son? Isn't Mary known to be his mother . . ." (see Matt. 13:55; Mark 6:3; John 6:42).

For the existential faith of those who are on fire for the Kingdom, recognizing that God is absolutely present in Jesus means that God is present in all those who are "excluded" from history. That gives rise to the extraordinary revolution that the experience of the incarnation introduces into human relationship with God. At the center of the mystery of the incarnation, a mystery that is salvation for the whole human race, the New Testament places man and woman, Jesus and Mary, God taking human flesh *in* and *by means of* woman's flesh, "born of a woman."

In the Gospel of Matthew also we can see Mary's divine motherhood affirmed. In the pericope of the angel's message to Joseph (1:18–25) it is said that the child who will be born from Mary's womb "will save his people from their sins" (v. 21). The expression "his people" is another reminder of the divine condition of the one who is to be born. The people to be saved is the same people chosen by God that the Old Testament calls "the people of Yahweh." According to the New Testament, this people is faithful to the Old Testament legacy, but is also open to the good news of the coming of the Messiah — it is the people of Jesus, and hence a new people, made up of Jews and pagans, that belongs to the Father and to the Son. All this — the salvation of the new people, the new Israel in person, who is Jesus, God made flesh — now grows in and emerges from the womb of Mary, a figure symbolizing the faithful people of Yahweh, who longingly await their redemption and accept the good news.

In the opening chapters of Luke, the most meaningful Old Testament symbols are used to describe Mary's divine motherhood. Just as the cloud accompanying the people and covering the tent of the covenant (Exod. 40:34) signifies that it is filled with the glory of Yahweh, so the power of the Spirit of the Most High, descending over Mary, causes her womb to be full of the presence of a Being who will be called Holy — Son of God.

Thus, according to Luke, Mary's divine motherhood becomes the new ark of the Covenant. The narrative of the visit to Elizabeth (Luke 1:39–44, 56), which follows that of the annunciation, reaffirms this symbolism. Jesus, the new alliance of God in person with human beings, now has in Mary his ark and dwelling. Just as in the second book of Samuel (2 Sam. 6:2–16) the Ark of the Covenant is carried and travels from Baala of Judah to Jerusalem, there to be received by the people with rejoicing and exultation, greeted with music and praise, recognized as the presence of blessing and venerated with holy awe, so Mary, the new ark, journeys to the house of Elizabeth, is greeted with leaps of joy by the child in her cousin's womb, and is acclaimed as blessed and venerated in her motherhood as "the Mother of the Lord" (see Luke 1:43).

It is this rich biblical vein that the councils took up and that the church developed from the time when it became necessary to clarify certain controverted points of doctrine on the mystery of the incarnation of Jesus Christ, his person, or his divine and human nature.

The only reference to Mary in the First Council of Constantinople is what is said of Jesus, repeating the Nicene Creed: "*Incarnatus est de Spiritu Sancto et Maria Virgine*" (He was incarnated of the Holy Spirit and the Virgin Mary).[8] Although this is not a direct statement about Mary's virginal motherhood, the assertion about her maternal function in the incarnation of the Son is quite explicit and firm. The fact that the assertion begins with the causal proposition *de* (*de Spiritu Sancto et Maria Virgine*) connects the explicit action of the Word (*incarnatus est*) to the Holy Spirit and to the Virgin Mary as to a single composite principle, divine and human. The person of Mary is united to the Holy Spirit grammatically and doctrinally as human co-principle in the process of the saving incarnation of God. Thus the formulation of Constantinople brings together both aspects of the mystery of Mary's divine motherhood: the ontological aspect, that is, her maternal function in the incarnation of the Son of God as such, and the soteriological aspect, the very purpose of the incarnation, which is "for the salvation of the human race."

The Council of Ephesus expressly declared that Mary is *Theotokos* (= Mother of God). The unity of two natures through the hypostasis of the Word and the interchangeability of attributes between Christ's two natures had been disputed. In this context, the question of Mary's divine motherhood came to the fore as a key for interpreting the mystery of the incarnation, which explains and makes possible the union of the two natures. As it became clear that the Word was begotten in a human manner, that is, the Word was conceived and born "of woman," the deep reasons for the divine motherhood emerged: what is said to be born of woman according to the flesh, in the sense that it has united human nature to itself hypostatically, is the Word eternally begotten by the Father; this is not an ordinary man into whom the Word of God, called the first-born according to the flesh, was subsequently inserted. Thus the council can call Mary the *Theotokos* (generator of God). As a result of this solemn proclamation and its glorious content the divine motherhood has since Ephesus been a unique title of dignity and glory for the one who is mother of the incarnate Word.

The Council of Chalcedon gave more formal and juridical clothing, that is, verbal form with a greater and more explicit dogmatic weight, to what Ephesus had solemnly declared to be a doctrine of faith. The conciliar text referring to divine motherhood reads: "the Son [is] born of the Father before all times as to his divinity, born in recent times for us and for our salvation from the Virgin Mary, Mother of God [*Deipara*],[9] as to his humanity" (DS 301, TCC 252). The wealth of Chalcedon consists in its affirmation of the divine motherhood of the Incarnate Word in terms that, for the sake of the incarnation, emphasize the bodily and human dimension, against the Monophysites who speak of Christ's flesh as a heavenly flesh, fruit of the work of the Holy Spirit, thus making Mary's motherhood unreal. The title *Virgin* alongside the expression *Deipara* ratifies and underscores the truth of this statement by asserting the full motherhood of her who gave birth to God. In this assertion that Mary's motherhood is genuine and true, she becomes the guarantee and the key for interpreting and verifying the oneness of the Word's being in his human generation.

In our day, Vatican II returned to the church's official discourse on Mary as Mother of God, dedicating a whole chapter of its most important document, the dogmatic constitution, *Lumen Gentium,* to her (chapter 8). There the divine motherhood is seen to be the doctrinal pivotal point for the entire mystery and mission of Mary, the whole of Marian theology in embryonic form. However, the council especially highlights the soteriological dimension of this motherhood. The council re-reads the mystery of the *Theotokos* proclaimed and revered by the church in the early centuries not so much for what it means in itself and in relation to Mary as an individual person or to the person of the Incarnate Word in themselves, but rather for the meaning that this motherhood gives to human salvation as a whole. Thus in her very divine motherhood Mary is a figure of the church. Mary's divine motherhood cannot be regarded as a single datum from the past, related only to Mary, but rather it is something renewed in all ages of salvation that take place in the church. Further, the divine motherhood establishes not only a close relationship between Mary and the church, but also between Mary and the people of God, which must be understood in its wider sense as encompassing the whole history of salvation. The Mother of God is also the servant of the Lord who puts her motherhood at the service of the salvation of the people. Thus the church is also called to be a servant and to place its saving treasure of revelation and faith, which it holds in trust, at the service of the world and of the human race.

The Marian theology drawn from this mystery of divine motherhood—a mystery the church has proclaimed a dogma of faith—can shed light on our situation today. Recognizing Mary as Mother of God really means professing that Jesus, the carpenter from Nazareth, the crucified one, son of Mary by human generation, is Son of God and very God. The term "God" here obviously applies only to the person of the Son and not to the Father or to the Holy Spirit. The Son is not on that account, however, less God, but fully and truly God. The anthropological vision that underlies this statement is therefore deeply holistic and unifying. Every woman is mother not only of the body but of the whole person of her child. In Jesus Christ humanity and divinity cannot be separated. In his person it is God who is living and acting in human flesh. Hence, neither in Mary can we separate the humble woman of Nazareth and she whom the church venerates and honors as Mother of God. The mystery of Jesus' incarnation in Mary's flesh teaches us that the human person is not split into a body of matter and imperfection, and a spirit of greatness and transcendence. Rather it is just in the frailty, poverty, and limits of human flesh that the ineffable greatness of the Spirit can be experienced and adored. The divine presence that the people of Israel adored and acclaimed in the Ark of the Covenant and to which only the high priest had access must now be adored and acclaimed in the face and body of every human being who, from the moment when the Word became flesh in Mary of Nazareth, is the dwelling place of the Spirit of God.

To proclaim Mary as Mother of God also means proclaiming the arrival of the Kingdom which is "already in your midst" (see Luke 17:21; Mt. 4:17; etc.). To confess that God indeed has taken flesh like ours, has joined our race, in the womb of a woman, is to state that the new reality of salvation— the Kingdom of God—has arrived for all those who belong to that same race. God has taken on human history from within, experiencing its struggles and achievements, defeats and victories, insecurities and joys. Mary is figure and symbol of the believing people that experiences this coming of God who now belongs to the human race. In her divine motherhood she is also the one who gives birth to Jesus, the Kingdom in person, and who continues to give birth to the Kingdom community, the new people, made up of all those who believe in and follow Jesus. Hence the scope of her motherhood is not only ontological, but because of everything that being mother of the savior God entails, it is also soteriological and universal in extent. She whose flesh formed the flesh of the Son of God is also the symbol and prototype of the new community where men and women love one another and celebrate the mystery of life in fulfillment made manifest.

To proclaim Mary Mother of God also means unveiling all the greatness of the mystery of woman: mystery of openness, source of life and protection for life. Since the creation account woman is linked to the begetting of life. She is Eve in the totality of her being—mother of the living, mother of life. Thus women—in alliance and complicity with life in their very being as women—are familiar with the conditions that life demands in its slow gestation, in the way its moments are drawn out, in the gradual way its fruitfulness blooms.[10] Very early the church saw in the woman Mary the New Eve—she who gives a new and decisively broad dimension to the mystery of woman's potency for motherhood. Mother of Jesus—the New Israel—Mary is also mother of all the living, woman in whom the mystery of the source and origin of life reaches its point of greatest intensity. Thus she reveals an unexperienced and unexplored side of the mystery of God incarnate in her womb: God who is life and life in abundance; God who in biblical revelation uses the image of a woman giving birth (see Isa. 66:13; 42:14) and of a woman who nurses the child of God's own womb and does not forget that child (Isa. 49:15); God whose face is shown in Mary of Nazareth and who takes her flesh for God's flesh in the Son Jesus; God whose face is manifested in every woman in this world, each of whom, in overcoming the signs of death and sterility, is custodian of hope and faith in life.

Finally, to proclaim that Mary is Mother of God with all the doxological and cultic resonances of that expression also entails recognizing, in her whom we call Our Mother and Our Lady, the poor and obscure woman of Nazareth, the mother of the subversive carpenter who was sentenced to death, Jesus. It entails recognizing that as regards Mary the theological title "Servant of the Lord" is just as real as the title of glory and the fancy images with which traditional piety represents her.

Scripture and the church's tradition understand Mary's divine motherhood as a gift and an honor but also as a service. This service is akin to that of the "servants of Yahweh." This is a service to the whole human race, which entails giving up one's life and a loving and total openness to the needs of others. In the Old Testament the faithful remnant of Israel is this servant who bears the infirmities and sins of the people so that redemption and salvation may come to this same people. Deutero-Isaiah personifies this collective figure of the Suffering Servant in an individual (Isa. 52–3), in whom the early Christian community in its re-reading saw the features of Jesus. In this tradition stands the motherhood of Mary, servant of the Lord (Luke: 1:38) in whom the Word of God is fulfilled and from whose pregnant body emerges the salvation and redemption of the people. The church, which sees in Mary its own figure and model, is called to set itself in this tradition. This church is called to be the servant of the Lord and to put itself at the service of all those today who suffer any kind of injustice, illness, and oppression. Especially in Latin America with its injustice and dire poverty, this church understands itself as church of the poor, for whom Jesus' incarnation in Mary has brought the good news of liberation.

3. A VIRGIN NAMED MARY

The dogma of Mary's virginity, which is quite closely connected to that of her divine motherhood, shows up differently in scripture and in the course it has taken in the church's tradition. It is a delicate subject and hard to approach, especially in today's world where sexual liberation and the findings of modern psychology raise serious questions about whether virginity is positive at all. Nevertheless, theology cannot evade this issue. We can attempt Marian theology only if we are willing to confront the dogma of Mary's virginity head on and ask: What historical grounds do we have for affirming it? What is the biblical basis for this dogma? Is this something central for Christian faith or not? What relevance can it have for the life of faith of men and women living here and now, at this time and in this place?

First of all, we must not forget that to approach Mary's virginal conception of Jesus means approaching mystery: the larger mystery of God's incarnation. Hence, it demands from us all the respect, veneration, and reverence that mystery demands, as we imbibe from the gospels and in the witness of faith, with the aid of the Holy Spirit, what we have indeed received from God. With this inner attitude and these dispositions, let us then approach the historic context in which the Gospels place this event of the virginal conception of Jesus.

Judaism, to which both Mary and Joseph fully belonged, did not see any special value in virginity. It was equivalent to sterility, not bearing offspring, which brought disdain and entailed a good measure of mortality, since survival was in one's offspring. For the Jewish woman not to be a mother therefore meant not being fulfilled as a woman.[11] When they sought to describe the misery of the people in the darkest manner the prophets said that the people was like a virgin who will die without leaving any descendants (see Amos 5:1–2; Jer.: 1:15; 2:13; Joel 1:8).

Nevertheless, even within Israel where this attitude prevailed, the Bible presents some exceptions where sterility in different forms (virginity, celibacy, widowhood) takes on a positive aspect of closer union with God and more radical service to God. There is the case of Moses who, after the Lord appeared to him on Mount Sinai (Deut. 5:30–31), stopped having relations with his wife Zipporah because the Lord had spoken to him "face to face" (Num. 12:8).[12] There is also the case of Jeremiah, who took on the celibate state as a prophetic sign to denounce the desolation and ruin of Israel (Jer. 16:1–9). The book of Wisdom praises the sterile woman and the eunuch who lived in a holy manner (Wis. 3:13–14; 4:1). Moreover, most importantly, the Bible expresses the belief and faith that God is the God of life and can make life spring forth where it would be impossible for a human creature. Thus, God's action made women like Sarah, Rebecca, Rachel, Samson's mother, Hannah, and Elizabeth fruitful. They became aware of the grace they had been given and broke into shouts of joy and songs of thanksgiving.

The New Testament texts that speak directly about Mary's virginity are few and contested exegetically. However, it is over these texts that theology must first ponder in order to drink from the mystery flowing from them. There is Paul's text, which we have already frequently cited, referring to Jesus, the Son of God, sent in the fullness of time as one "born of woman" (Gal. 4:4). Here the reference to virginity is not really explicit, but it can be indirectly deduced and understood within the larger mystery of *kenosis* — the descent and humiliation of the Son of God who "is born of woman and under the law." Mark's Gospel refers to Jesus as "the son of Mary" (Mark 6:3), even though according to biblical custom it would be more logical to mention the father rather than the mother, as Matthew and Luke do (Matt. 13:55; Luke 3:23), calling him respectively the "son of the carpenter," and the "son — so it was supposed — of Joseph." There is a great deal of discussion about whether an expression in the fourth Gospel (1:13) is to be understood in the singular: "they who were (he who was) begotten . . . not by carnal desire, nor by man's willing it, but by God." If it is singular, the text may refer to the Word, conceived by the Holy Spirit in the virginal womb of Mary, "begotten by God."

It is Matthew and Luke who treat the question of Mary's virginity most directly. Matthew 1:18 says that before she had lived together with Joseph, Mary was found "with child through the Holy Spirit." That statement is then reaffirmed in the announcement made to Joseph on the mysterious pregnancy of his spouse which so perplexed him (v. 20). Pointedly, the text continues: "[Joseph] received her into his home as his wife. He had no relations with her at any time before she bore a son, whom he named Jesus" (vv. 24–5). In Luke the key statement on the fact of virginal conception is again as in Matthew completely enshrouded in pneumatological mystery. To the astonishment of Mary, who is troubled over how she might conceive since she "does not know man," the angel solemnly declares: "The Holy

Spirit will come upon you and the power of the Most High will overshadow you; hence, the holy offspring to be born will be called Son of God" (Luke 1:34–5). From a theological stand-point, it is striking to see how these two writers use the Greek words (to "beget," which is closer to the male element in con-ception; to "deliver," female, to give birth). Matthew says of Mary that "she is to give birth to a son" (1:21) and that "she gave birth to a son" (1:25) without Joseph having relations with her. In Matthew's Gospel, Jesus is "the one who was born," and this is announced as heavenly revelation to Joseph by the angel and to the magi through the star (2:2). In his genealogies Mat-thew says that "Jacob was the father of Joseph the husband of Mary, of whom Jesus called Christ *was begotten*" (1:16). Luke is also continually alert to how these words are used. While he speaks of Elizabeth as *bearing* her son John the Baptist (1:36), he says that Mary *gives birth* (2:7). When the the verb *beget* appears in connection with Mary it is used—as also in Mat-thew—in the passive impersonal: in reference to that which will be begotten (1:35).[13]

What can we say about Mary's virginity on the basis of what the Gospels tell us? How can we free ourselves of any kind of biologizing or psychologizing reductionism and try to move for-ward in the theological task before us? We can review the read-ing of the New Testament texts we have carried out in Chapter II. It is quite clear that the Gospels do not intend to give us a detailed description of the genetic and biological features sur-rounding the conception and birth of Jesus in order to satisfy our unhealthy curiosity. What they do seek to do, in keeping with their narrations as a whole, is to set before our eyes a sign that challenges our faith, going beyond our understanding. Like the miracles Jesus performed while moving through this world, this sign is not to be evaluated in itself, but rather points to something greater, to the wonders God is working for men and women out of love.

The first persistent convergence that appears in the texts on Mary's virginity is this: that the son begotten in her is a divine being.[14] It is no longer a question of God speaking "in fragmen-tary and varied ways" to the people (Heb. 1:1), but here it is God the Son made flesh, as a saving gift to the people and to the world. To affirm the virginity of the mother, who is the human origin of the Son of God, is to affirm alike the divine origin of this Son. In the texts this divine origin is not referred to the Father (male principle) but to the Holy Spirit, to the *ruach* in the Old Testament, the *pneuma* in the New Testament (Matt. 1:18–20; Luke 1:25), thus radically ruling out any attempt at a theogamic model.[15] There is a radical break in the chain of human genealogies in order to make way for the Spirit who comes into history with a creative breath and makes life spring forth where it was impossible. This is the same Spirit who changes dry bones into a militant army (Ezek. 37:12–14), who changes the desert into an orchard and the orchard into a forest (Isa. 32:15–17), who makes "life in abundance" (see John 10:10) spring from Mary's untouched womb. Hence, this is not an anthropological item of information about what happens on a narrowly personal level among God, a mother, and her son. Rather the virginal conception of Jesus in Mary opens the horizon to a new birth (see John 1:13) for men and women of all ages. Jesus, the New Israel who springs from the Virgin's womb, is the seed of the new people that is formed by the Spirit in the faithful people of which Mary is figure and symbol.

Church tradition took this biblical datum in a pure, indeed almost wild, state, and went on to proclaim its doctrine on Mary's virginity. The theological development of the early centuries of Christianity progressed to the point of firmly establishing theologically the fact that Mary is ever virgin.[16] The magisterium has also made pronouncements. While Chalcedon was satisfied with the formula "born of the Virgin Mary" the Second Council of Constantinople (533) brought in an explicit reference to perpetual virginity: "He was incarnated of the glorious *Theotokos* and ever Virgin Mary." The definition of Mary's perpetual virginity dates back to the Lateran Council (649), canon 3 of which says: "If any one do not truly and rightly confess with the fathers that the holy, ever virginal and immaculate Mary is *Mother of God,* since in recent days she really and truly conceived, without seed, by the Holy Ghost, the same divine Word who was born before all time and gave birth to him in chastity, her virginity remaining unimpaired after the birth — *condemnatus sit*" (DS 503, TCC 269).

So theology, catechesis, and pastoral work today face the challenge of having to transmit this truth of the faith to new generations, and in that task they run up against the mentality and values of today. Even in Brazil where the bulk of the people are full of strong devotion to Mary, it is not easy to talk about her virginity. What meaning can we see today in announcing the virginal motherhood of her whom Christian piety calls "the Virgin"?

As we explained in Chapter II, theologically speaking, virginity refers to the creation in Mary of a new people, a virgin people in the sense that it is not given over to idolatry, a people begotten by the "power of the Most High." From the viewpoint of theological anthropology, Mary's virginity points back to a deep, vital experience: that of questioning who the human being is in God's presence. Standing before the One who is the Most High and in the shadow of whose power we stand, who is the human person? Mary's virginity answers this question for us without claiming to give an account of the mystery that continues to surround it. Rather her virginity draws us back to the beginning of the world and to the birth of creation when, drawing the world out of primitive chaos, God forms out of clay a covenant partner, to God's image, male and female — creature.

Thus the human creature, standing before the One who created it, is like virgin unexplored land, where *anything* can happen. And anything that happens should lead this same human creature to where Mary arrived: to have formed God within oneself. The virginity of Mary made fruitful by the Spirit of the Most High is paralleled by the vocation of every human being, called to be "clothed with power from on high" (Luke 24:49), "being formed into Christ" (see Phil. 3:10), "temple of the Holy Spirit" (see 1 Cor. 6:19).

In her pregnant virginity, Mary is what humankind is called to be from the creation: temple and dwelling place, open and available, with all possibilities latent, like a blank page ready for the writings of the Spirit so as to become "a letter of Christ" (see 2 Cor. 3:3), image of God.

Instead of providing biological information, therefore, the biblical account points us toward a theological path that leads to faith in the Savior God through the witness of the primitive community. Mary's virginity highlights God's right of self-communication with God's people not only through words, but also through tangible and concrete deeds that allow the people to comprehend and "touch" the salvation it is being offered. Just as God's gift to the people—Jesus—does not come from the erotic relationship of two human partners but from the power of the Most High, so also salvation is not immanent within human beings, but is a gratuitous gift to be received in humility and faith. The "impotence" of Mary's virgin body is a figure of humankind's poverty when it comes to achieving its own salvation without God's grace. When the people withdraw from God, their history is a succession of false turns, failures, confusions. When they assent and allow themselves to be shaped by the Spirit, the bones stand up, the desert blooms, the virgin conceives. Mary's virginity is therefore a sign of the sovereignty of God who comes near in grace and enables men and women to build toward the Kingdom.

This God who speaks and acts with the people in this manner is not far off and indifferent, but is, on the contrary, a jealous God, jealous (Exod. 34:14) of her whom he has chosen to be his beloved wife, Israel, his vineyard, his love. God wants to be the only one for her, and does not allow her the right to any infidelity to the covenant they have made, or to any sort of idolatry. In this biblical context, Mary's virginity is not regarded as an individualistic and exclusive privilege, but rather as a prototypical affirmation of the qualities and attitude required of the new people toward the Spirit and toward God's covenant which comes toward human flesh.[17] Total commitment to the God of life and radical rejection of the idols that bring death lead to seeing in Mary's virginity a figure proposed for all, men and women, married and celibate, who want to follow in Jesus' footsteps and live out the historic and eschatological reality of the Kingdom of God.[18]

The mystery of Mary's virginity also tells us something about the mystery of woman. Returning once more to the creation account in the first chapter of Genesis, we can see that—according to the priestly source—when God creates the human being (Adam) to God's image, that being is created man and *negevah* (= woman) (Gen. 1:27).

Negevah means the woman who is "crossed through" or "transfixed." One who can be crossed through or transfixed is an open being, a being with space. Woman is thus basically the one where God dug and opened space. He made her openness, space for freedom to choose, protect, nourish, and preserve; discreet and secret space for enveloping mystery; available and virgin space ready to host all possibilities, all horizons of life. Facing that life that is God, woman is that "ontological openness,"[19] that virginity ready to be run through by the power of the Most High and fecundated with the Word of life.

Hence Mary's virginity beckons not only insofar as every human creature is called to be more, but it particularly points toward woman's vocation as she is host of life in fullness, as she is boundlessly open, as she is the hidden potential that grows in proportion to the depth of her commitment. That vocation, symbolized in woman's physical make-up, does not rule out men sharing in it, but the feminine symbolism is more evocative in this respect. Far from limiting and reducing woman to sterility, far from denying her sexuality, the dogma of Mary's virginity forever declares a positive space where the Spirit of the Most High can repose and have a dwelling. In the Bible the Holy Spirit finds a definitive human vessel only once — and that vessel is Mary's virginity. Hence once and for all there is sealed a symbolic affinity of woman with the Spirit, who is "Lord and source of life," who is in God's covenant with humankind and in the mystery of the very inner life of God, the one who is at the beginning and at the end as the life-giving and glorifying principle.[20] The mystery of woman finds in the paradoxical mystery of Mary's virginity a trace of her own unrestricted and unlimited vocation.

Mary's virginity is therefore not simply a genital or sexual matter or an amazing exceptional case of parthenogenesis; nor does it entail disdain for sexuality and marriage. It is emphatically a message of deepest significance, utterly in agreement with the good news of the gospel and with the way God tends to act with God's people. Besides what has been said already, Mary's virginity is about the glory of the almighty God made manifest in what is poor, impotent, and disdained in the eyes of the world. The virginity looked down upon in Israel is the site for the

Shekinah, the dwelling-place of Yahweh's glory. God's preference for the poor becomes clear and explicit when God becomes
incarnate in a virgin's womb. Hence Mary sings the great things
that the Powerful One, who has seen the servant's lowliness, has
done in her (Luke 1:48, 59). Society and religion should not
esteem her virginity for ascetic reasons; rather, like her motherhood, her virginity points toward service to the poor of Yahweh, those men and women who with empty hands and willing
hearts every day lift their faces and repeat, "I am the servant of
the Lord. Let it be done to me as you say" (Luke 1:38).

4. FULL OF GRACE: THE IMMACULATE CONCEPTION

The dogma of Mary's immaculate conception has a complex
history in the church. Starting from an almost total silence in
the Bible and the oldest tradition, it follows an up-and-down
course until the moment of a solemn dogmatic definition in 1854.
This process shows the importance for the life of the church of
what is called the *sensus fidelium,* that is, the shared sense of
the faithful toward certain truths of the faith not officially proclaimed by the magisterium. The church's faith matures and
grows in its understanding of what has been revealed under the
influence of the Spirit and through the exercise of the various
charisms (*Dei Verbum* 8).

Pius IX proclaimed the dogma of the immaculate conception
in 1854 at the height of modernism in society and culture and
when anti-modernism held sway in the church. At that time the
institutional church feared the advance of modernist ideas, the
progress of the sciences in general, and especially of political
science as represented in socialist ideas then breaking out in
Europe and threatening the religious world of Catholicism.

To some extent the declaration that Mary was exempt from
original sin served to reaffirm the church's stance of unwilling-
ness to be involved with modernism, which was regarded as the
great sin of that period. Without setting aside the theological
truth of the dogma we are attempting to explain, we need to see
how through it the church intended to say something circumstantial, though true and definitive, to the world.

From the very beginnings of the church, popular faith has

played a very important role in establishing what would subsequently become the dogma of the immaculate conception. As far back as the second century, the apocryphal Gospel of James included a story from popular circles about the conception of Mary by Anne, her mother, already advanced in years, without the intervention of man. Although there are no statements about this in the councils of the first few centuries, many of the church's fathers are unending in their praise for Mary and call her most holy. In his controversy with the Pelagians Augustine goes so far as to say that "piety demands that we recognize Mary as without sin" and that "for the sake of the Lord's honor" Mary in no way "comes under consideration with regard to sin."[21] In the next few centuries one can see a division between popular faith—which stood on the side of the immaculate conception—and a portion of more learned theology that stood opposed. Finally in the nineteenth century, when a combination of events overcame the theological obstacles, Pius IX published the bull *Ineffabilis Deus* (December 8, 1854) saying that in doing so he was "satisfying the deepest desire of the Catholic world." Here is a bit of the text:

> We ... declare, pronounce and define that the doctrine which holds that the Most Blessed Virgin Mary from the first moment of her conception was, by the singular grace and privilege of Almighty God, in view of the merits of Christ Jesus the Saviour of the human race, preserved immune from all stain of original sin, is revealed by God and is therefore firmly and constantly to be believed by all the faithful. (DS 2803, TCC 325)

The people's deep intuition in faith, worship, and practice led the magisterium to make a clear pronouncement and define a dogma. Theology, which at some points along the way resisted this popular desire, today feels called to carry out its proper role in the church community, that of pondering this dogmatic definition and trying to enter within it and assess how firm its roots are, without, however, exhausting the mystery whose totality belongs to God alone.

Although dogma is not a repetition of scripture it is not a

new revelation either: it is a homogeneous development— perceived by the instinct of faith—of everything that is already within the overall horizon of revelation. Thus it is not enough to find a basis just in the person of Mary or in the a priori of her motherhood or virginity and from that point deduce the statement that she was preserved from sin, which is part of the human condition from the beginning. We must turn our eyes to the data of revelation we have—however scarce they may be— and try to relate this information to the intuition of the people's faith, which has proclaimed the absolute sanctity of the mother of Jesus from the start.

In order to move a little further into this mystery of Mary's ontological sanctity—the immaculate conception—we cannot seek the biblical datum in a pure state. We must always take it up in connection with the reading the church and tradition have made of it. In this reading we can recognize some biblical texts that enable us to pick out Mary's immaculate conception, albeit in seed form.

The first such text is Genesis 3:15 (also called the proto-gospel), where the woman and her offspring are seen to be mortal enemies of the serpent, which they eventually destroy, stamping on its head. Thus the woman Mary is said to be the personification of good struggling against evil. Next there is a whole series of biblical figures that the fathers of the church very often applied to Mary: the ark of Noe (Gen. 6:8–8:19), Jacob's ladder (Gen. 28:12), the impregnable tower (Song of Sol. 4:4), the enclosed garden (Song of Sol. 4:12), the shining city of God (Jerusalem), whose foundations are on the holy mountain (Ps. 87:1, 3), God's temple, filled with the glory of the Lord (1 Kgs. 8:10–11). The fathers use images from prophetic writings and other texts to celebrate Mary: "pure dove" (Song of Sol. 2:10, 14; 5:2; 6:9), Holy Jerusalem (Ps. 87), God's high throne (Eccles. 42:2), ark made holy (Exod. 25:10; 40:34–35; 1 Kgs. 8:10–11; Ezek. 43:1–5), house that eternal wisdom has built for itself (Prov. 9:1), and queen who, filled with delights and depending on her beloved (Song of Sol. 8:5), comes from the mouth of the Most High absolutely perfect, beautiful, most beloved by God and ever-preserved from the stain of guilt (Eccles. 24:3).

Thus, in the patristic reading of the Old Testament, Mary is seen as this "dwelling of God," this pure and receptive site where God can enter and remain in all glory and majesty without encountering any opposition or resistance. The symbolism of most Old Testament figures points to this idea: ark, city, house, garden.

The two New Testament texts that most stand out are the angel's greeting (Luke 1:28 "full of grace") and Elizabeth's blessing (Luke 1:42: "Blest are you among women and blest is the fruit of your womb"). Thus among all God's creatures Mary is viewed as the one closest to God. She is God's miracle par excellence, creation come to fulfillment, blessed, most favored, full of grace.

We can see that scripture, as this quick review of the texts shows, when read with the eyes of the church, reveals a certain coherence of meaning that does not come directly from the letter pure and simple. What the people of God have intuited from the beginning, theology seeks to work out laboriously, plumbing the mysterious wealth of the texts in order to advance the thinking and faith of the community.

In our view, Mary's immaculate conception must be considered in connection with the people of which she is figure and symbol and in relation to God in whom Mary believes and who chooses her and gives her a particular vocation and mission within salvation history.

As "daughter of Zion" Mary is the incarnation of the Jewish people from which she descends and to which she is closely connected. With her the journey of this people on the way toward the Messiah who is the fullness of time comes to its destination. Israel, God's chosen people, is more particularly that people in whose midst God resides and dwells by means of the temple. Jerusalem, the holy city which after the trials of exile once more takes on and represents the community of the chosen people, is the beloved spouse of Yahweh her husband. All her infidelities are redeemed by this God, whose love is more powerful than anything else. Her afflictions are turned into joy by the presence of the husband. Mary personifies and sums up the ancient Zion-Jerusalem. In her the process of renewal and purification of the whole people of God—a process that has as its goal that the people will live the alliance with God more fully—finds a model beginning. Wholly belonging to God, Mary is prototype of what the people is called to be, chosen "in him before the world began, to be holy and blameless" (Eph. 1:4).

The full identity of the people, given by God in creation and election and lost in the people's infidelity and exile, is restored by God in a "new creation," as it were, with the advent of new heavens and a new earth (Isa. 65:17; 66:22). In Mary this new creation actually takes place. She is the figure of the re-created people, filled and overflowing with the glory and power of Yahweh, pregnant with the promised Messiah who has now been sent. The time in which God's presence and holiness were restricted to the stone temple in Jerusalem is drawing to a close. Now, in the fullness of time, human flesh is God's temple. It is in the flesh of the woman Mary, full of grace, pregnant with the man Jesus, that the fullness of divine holiness is found in the world. It is in the flesh of every man and every woman who belong to the same race as Jesus and Mary that God must be sought, respected, venerated, and adored. What the chosen people sees about itself in the scene where it receives the law on Sinai, that moment when it says a wife's yes to her husband, that moment of the covenant for which the groom has lovingly prepared and guided the bride—the church says that this has become completely true in the person of Mary, the "Lord's handmaid."

The immaculate conception is therefore a utopia that energizes that people's overall endeavor and sustains their hope in their God (see Puebla 298). At the end of a long history of grace and sin, of love and passion, is the woman inaugurating a new era which already bears within itself the anticipation of the end, when God will be all in all. In the figure of Mary, the church, the new people of God, sees its yearnings and longings, the divine proposal for humankind, already achieved. "Mary is presented as the culmination of humankind and Israel's crowning glory. . . . History runs out and humankind rests because in its own representative it sees itself transported to the fulfillment of history, when utopia will become reality."[22] Mary's immaculate conception is the pledge that assures that Jesus' utopia—the Kingdom of God—can be achieved on this poor earth.

The dogma of the immaculate conception also tells us that it is not only Mary's *soul* that is preserved from sin and from being contrary to God's design. It is her whole person that is permeated and stimulated by grace, by God's life, and it is her bodiliness that is the dwelling place of God most holy, the soil in which the incarnate Word sprouts forth, the place where the Holy Spirit rests and pitches tent. Mary's immaculate conception tells the people of which she is a figure that the Spirit has been poured forth over all flesh and that the paradise lost has been found once more. Humankind, to which Mary fully belongs, has produced an unpoisoned fruit, a daughter, who even though she is the dwelling place for the splendor of the Spirit, "remains anchored in the earth, in history, in the concreteness of the human condition."[23]

The gospel and the magisterium rehabilitate woman's bodiliness, which Genesis denounced as the cause of original sin, laying on women a blemish and a burden that were difficult to bear. It is this body animated by the divine Spirit that is proclaimed blessed. In it God works the fullness of God's wonders. It is in the flesh and the person of a woman that humankind can see its call and its destiny brought to a happy end.

Finally, and most important, we cannot forget that the immaculate conception venerated on our altars is the poor Mary of Nazareth, Handmaid of the Lord, Mother of the People, insignificant in the social structure of her time. The prototypical figure in whom the blessings of the Sermon on the Mount are embodied, blessed Mary, as Elizabeth and all generations call her (Luke 1:42–43), bears within herself the confirmation of God's preference for the humblest, the littlest, and the most oppressed. The so-called Marian privilege is really the privilege of the poor. The grace of which Mary is full is the inheritance of the whole people. More than ever Mary—the *tapeinē*[24] of Nazareth—on whom the gaze of the Most High rests with favor, is a model for the church, stimulating it to become more and more the church of the poor.

5. VICTORIOUS AND OUR LADY: THE ASSUMPTION

The most recent of the Marian dogmas is the assumption. Solemnly defined and proclaimed by Pius XII on November 1,

1950, with the apostolic constitution *Munificentissimus Deus* (MD), it is one of the three Marian feasts in the liturgical year and is celebrated on August 15.

The point in history when the dogma of Mary's assumption was defined and proclaimed is not unimportant for understanding the dogma itself. It was 1950 and the church was at the very center of a world weakened and shaken by two world wars. Europe, the center of so-called Western Christian civilization, was groaning in humiliation over the ruin of its past splendor. At that moment, Pius XII proclaimed the dogma of Mary's assumption and it resounded in the ears of the world like a profession of faith in humanity. The very humankind that no longer believed in itself could channel the potential of the faith it still retained toward her who is its most worthy representative and see her, victorious, together with God, and in this way regain hope in its own future.

The document defining and explaining the theological and vital meaning of the dogma of the assumption provides a biblical foundation. This foundation, however, does not use the letter of the texts as its starting point, but rather the scripture as already interpreted by the great tradition of the church: the fathers, the theologians, the great preachers, who "to illustrate their faith in the assumption utilize the data and statements of scripture with a certain freedom." That is, they use scripture texts to show how this privilege of Mary "is admirably in agreement with the truths taught in Sacred Scripture."[25] Thus Pius XII sees scripture as the "ultimate foundation" of the divinely revealed dogma that "the immaculate Mother of God, Mary ever Virgin, when the course of her earthly life was finished, was taken up body and soul into the glory of heaven" (DS 3903, TCC 334c).

The first text MD takes up is the *proto-evangelium,* which speaks about the mortal enmity between the serpent, author of death, and the woman, defender of life. Mary, the New Eve, closely connected to the New Adam who is Jesus Christ in this struggle against the infernal enemy, is, together with Christ, victorious over that enemy. "Hence as the glorious resurrection of Christ was an essential part and the final sign of this victory, in like manner the struggle which the Blessed Virgin endured in common with her Son was to end in the 'glorification' of her virginal body" (DS 3901, TCC 334b). Thus MD sees the assumption of Mary as the outcome of a life totally devoted to God and others, in radical opposition to anything that is sin, which diminishes life. Sharing with the Son in struggle and suffering, she also shares with him in glory. The Pauline writings on the resurrection as victory over sin and death (Rom. 5–6; 1 Cor. 15:21–26, 54–57) are cited to support this line of argument.

The constitution invokes countless other texts, of which we single out those we see as more important:

—*Psalm 131(132):8:* "Advance, O Lord, to your resting place, you and the ark of your majesty." The fathers and theologians of the church have traditionally seen the image of the Ark of the Covenant, site of the divine presence, as an image of Mary. Even the Old Testament hints at this re-reading when it speaks of the Ark of the Covenant. Inside the ark, which was made of wood, were carried the two tablets of the law that Moses received from the Lord on Mount Sinai, when the covenant was concluded with the people. The ark is regarded as a privileged symbol of God's presence (*Shekinah*) in the midst of the people. Insofar as it is God's presence within God's people the ark is incorruptible. Because God's covenant with Israel is eternal, the ark cannot perish. Mary—ark of the new and eternal covenant of God with humankind, the place where God made flesh has reposed—is glorified without experiencing corruption. Hence the words of the psalm read from this angle sing the reality of the Lord—the new covenant— glorified together with Mary, she who was the Lord's place and dwelling on this earth.

—*Luke 1:28:* The scholastic doctors saw in the angel's greeting in Luke's Gospel—which the faithful around the world have said in the Hail Mary: "Rejoice, you who are full of grace, the Lord is with you . . ."—a path leading to what later, in MD, became the dogma of the assumption. In this mystery of Mary's glorious assumption, the church has seen, as it were, the complement to the Virgin Mary's fullness of grace and a singular blessing that stands in opposition to Eve's curse.[26] The dogma of the assumption is thus closely connected to the other Marian dogmas: the one assumed into heaven, victorious and Our Lady, is the Virgin who opened herself to the Word and was fruitfully impregnated by the Spirit; she is the Mother who out of her own flesh formed the flesh of the very Word of life and who was acclaimed by a simple ordinary woman (Luke 11:27–8); she is the one immaculately conceived, full of grace, full of God; with her the Lord is continually beginning the new creation.

—*Revelation 12:* The fathers and theologians of the church see Mary's assumption announced not only in the various Old Testament figures and symbols and in the Gospels, but also in the woman in Revelation 12, dressed in the sun, full of light,[27] over whom the shades of death no longer have power. Mother of him whom the first witnesses saw as the "light of the world" Mary participates intimately in the glory of the Son, just as she has participated in his life, persecution, and death.

Although it is indirect this biblical basis was the beginning of a long process gradually extending over twenty centuries of church history and culminating in the 1950 proclamation. Above all else the path traversed was one of faith. Contending with obscure and contrasting aspects, with few and contradictory objective data, different generations of Christians opened the way for reflection on what their sense of faith told them about the mystery of the Mother of God.

The first hypotheses about Mary having a singular final destiny made their appearance around the fourth century, based on old apocryphal accounts.[28] From that point onward there was a long, winding journey, with the Protestant Reformation in the middle. Finally at the height of the post-war period, with many petitions coming from around the Catholic world urging that the dogma be defined, Pius XII went ahead with the solemn dogmatic definition.[29] The value of MD lies in the fact that it seeks to gather up not only the centuries-long advance of the whole church with regard to Mary's final destiny, but that it also attempts to draw up a critical summary of all the theological reflection carried out through the centuries of church history and passed on through the traditions of the fathers and doctors, through the liturgy, and through the collective sense of all the faithful; the apostolic constitution fulfills this tradition by declaring as a dogma of faith *"divinely revealed"* that Mary has been finally and definitively glorified. In doing so, the magisterium of the church appreciates and takes into account, as it did with the dogma of the immaculate conception, the universal faith testimony of the faithful, which taken as a whole can be regarded as a revelation of the Holy Spirit.

Does the task of theology end here? we ask. Once the church's highest doctrinal level has taken a stand, do not all the arguments and discussions cease, leaving theological reflection with nothing more to do but repeat what the official magisterium has already said? Yet if we see the dogmatic formulation as something living and real that is an integral part not only of an established body of doctrine set once and for all, but also of the very life of the church, which is dynamic and always in motion, it is especially important continually to re-read the implications that this truth of faith has for the faithful in every age and everywhere. The same is true of the dogma of Mary's assumption. What implications can it have for us today, here and now?

The very text of the definition already draws our attention in this sense when it says that "the immaculate Mother of God, Mary ever Virgin, when the course of her earthly life was finished, was taken up body and soul into the glory of heaven" (DS 3904, TCC 334c). The expression "body and soul" is basic. Out of the letter of the text there emerges a theological idea that is deep and sound. The subject of the assumption is not the body or soul of Mary of Nazareth, but

> Mary's *person* as a whole and understood as mother of God, immaculate and ever virgin, truths which are now firmly established in the faith of the church. Even if the formula does not use the possessive personal pronoun "her" when it points to the body and soul, it is clear that it assumes it, since it speaks of her glorification at the end of her earthly life, with a clear relation of continuity between Mary glorified in soul and body and Mary soul and body during her earthly life.[30]

This quote brings out the anthropology underlying the text, one that overcomes the dualism so often present in traditional Mariology. The apostolic constitution does not see Mary as a soul provisionally wrapped in a body of death, but as a person, a body animated by the divine Spirit, with God's grace extending to her every aspect. God fully assumes her bodiliness and assumes it to glory. Her assumption is not the re-animation of a corpse, or the exaltation of a soul separated from a body, but the complete fulfillment of the whole woman, Mary of Nazareth, in God's absoluteness. Mary's glorification is all-embracing and complete, including "her rootedness in the earth, her material and fleshly density, her relatedness to cosmos and history."[31] We who believe in Mary's assumption simultaneously profess our faith in the eschatological final destiny to which we are called. We are not a soul imprisoned in a body; nor is this body a hindrance to complete fulfillment as human beings or to our union with God. On the contrary, in the resurrection, our bodiliness, which during our earthly life is a factor of both power and frailty, is redeemed and transfigured within God's absoluteness. What we believe and hope is already fully achieved in Mary. That which was the site of God's incarnation blazes the trail so that all of us, following the Son, may have full access to the joyful existence God has prepared for those who love God (1 Cor. 2:9). In this way Mary's assumption tells us that anthropology leads to eschatology, and that a unifying and holistic anthropology unveils new and hope-inspiring horizons for the final destiny of human beings whom God so loves (see Puebla, 298).

In addition, the dogma of the assumption implies a new and decisive reversal of any possible false turns stemming from an individualistic anthropology. If, as we have been trying to say so far, Marian theology really must see in Mary not simply an individual, but a symbol-figure, a collective personality who points to a whole people, her assumption should also be seen from this angle. Glorified in heaven in body and soul, Mary, according to Vatican II (LG, 8), is image and beginning of the church of the future, eschatological sign of hope and consolation for the people of God journeying toward the light and toward its final homeland. This people, *already* redeemed and full of hope, but *still* journeying on the path of history, sees in Mary the concrete possibility of arriving at the Day of the Lord. Mary is an initial member of the church in history. She is not outside or above the church. Yet she represents the *figure* or *model* of the church; and as it acts in history, the church is called to draw inspiration for carrying out its mission from her, from her fidelity to God and to the people.

By pointing to Mary, assumed in glory as the beginning and image of the future eschatological church, spouse of the Lamb who will appear there without blemish or wrinkle, the church's magisterium is also saying that in Mary the future eschatological reality of the church is already beginning. With the assumption of Mary—figure and symbol of God's new people—the church *is already,* even in the midst of its ambiguity and its sin, the community of salvation, and the faithful people it is called to be. Mary's assumption is thus not something solitary, abstract, and alienating for God's people on the way, but a stimulus and a reference point that impel the people along that route of history which already contains within itself final eschatological perfection in embryonic form. Through her assumption, Mary herself remains in the world and within the church as someone who is living and intensely present, a living being with whom communication is possible, not only through remembrance and memory, but also through a relationship. The people of Latin America, simple and full of faith, are very much aware of this— they seek her out and consult with her in their doubts; they go to her with their needs; they journey miles and miles to stand for a minute before her image in one of her numerous shrines. "Alive in God," Mary, through her assumption, is the hope, the mother, the protector who does not forsake her children. She is equally the figure of the people experiencing even here and now the inexpressible reality of God's presence in their midst, the reality of the Kingdom.

Mary's assumption also brings a new and promising future for women. The fact that a woman participates—wholly and fully—in the glory of the living God means that the female body is rescued from all the humiliation that Judeo-Christian civilization has laid on it.

Excluded from Jewish initiation rites because of their anatomy, banned from full participation in worship and the synagogue by their menstrual cycles, for a long time women— even in Christianity—subtly or explicitly have been second-class citizens in the the world of faith because of the "inferiority" and the "poverty" of their bodies.

Mary's assumption restores and reintegrates woman's bodiliness into the very mystery of God. Starting with Mary, the
dignity of women's condition is recognized and safeguarded by
the Creator of that very bodiliness. In Jesus Christ and Mary
the feminine is respectively resurrected and assumed into
heaven — definitively sharing in the glory of the trinitarian mystery from which all proceeds and to which all returns.

Nevertheless, given the situation in the church and the world
when it was defined, Mary's assumption could seem to respond
more to a triumphalistic ecclesiology than to the desires and
intuitions of the poorest and humblest folk. Even Vatican II,
although it provided a new vision of Mariology by setting it in
the framework of salvation history and by placing it back where
it was in early tradition, does not offer many leads for a popular
Mariology sensitive to the problems of the poor.[32] Although that
is true of Mariology in general, it is even more true of the assumption. As a dogma that sets Mary in the bosom of God's
glory, making her Queen and Our Lady, might it not also distance her from the poor woman of Nazareth, with whom the
humblest people can identify?

Mary's assumption, however, is intimately connected to Jesus'
resurrection. Both events of faith are about the same mystery:
the triumph of God's justice over human injustice, the victory
of grace over sin. Just as proclaiming the resurrection of Jesus
means continuing to announce his passion which continues in
those who are crucified and suffer injustice in this world, by
analogy, believing in Mary's assumption means proclaiming that
the woman who gave birth in a stable among animals, whose
heart was pierced with a sword of sorrow, who shared in her
son's poverty, humiliation, persecution, and violent death, who
stood at the foot of the cross, the mother of the condemned,
has been exalted. Just as the crucified one is the risen one (see
Acts 2:22–4), so the sorrowing one is the one assumed into
heaven, the one in glory. She who, while a disciple herself,
shared persecutions, fear, and anxiety with other disciples in the
early years of the church, is the same one who, after a death
that was certainly humble and anonymous, was raised to heaven.
The assumption is the glorious culmination of the mystery of
God's preference for what is poor, small, and unprotected in

this world, so as to make God's presence and glory shine there. Mary's assumption—seen in the light of Jesus' resurrection—is hope and promise for the poor of all times and for those who stand in solidarity with them; it is hope and promise that they will share in the final victory of the incarnate God.

The resurrection is the interpretative word of the Father confirming the path Jesus has taken. The assumption is the word of the same God who in Mary is utterly grace and who confirms her journey. In doing so, God indicates to God's people the path to take, following Mary's example. For the church, people of God, Mary's assumption is a horizon of eschatological hope that points the church toward its place in the midst of the poor, of those at the edge, of all those whom society pushes aside. "Assumed in glory Mary continues her task of struggling against the structures of sin, a struggle she waged during her mortal life."[33] The virgin of the Magnificat—on whose lips is placed the message that God is exalting the humble and casting down the powerful—finds her life confirmed and glorified by the Father of Jesus. The church who sees in her its figure and model, "our life, sweetness, and hope," strives to live and follow this same path. The advocate of the poor, the consoler of the afflicted, the mother of the humble, is Our Lady, the triumphant one. In the option for the poor, and in zealous defense of the most unprotected and oppressed of humankind, the church in Latin America finds the way to participate in the glory of the Groom who continually comes out to meet her: "A Marian theology whose starting point is the poor cannot but help shape an image of the church of the poor, a church that is poor and of the people."[34]

It might be good to note at this point that we are not pausing here to consider the question of Mary co-redeemer and mediatrix, since we want to restrict our attention to the church's official dogmatic teaching.

6. THE DOGMATICS OF THE POOR

As the heir to Judaism, Christianity has been organized officially around the figure of Jesus Christ. Everything starts with

him and converges toward him, including theological reflection
on Mary.

For the various Christian churches, all theology, and Christology in particular, has been read and done against the backdrop of patriarchal culture, for which "man" is the model for
humanity.

Without denying the value and importance of this tradition,
especially since we have been shaped by it, it is important to
affirm other Christian traditions and to try to discover what they
say: that is, what aspect of divine-human reality they most emphasize. We would particularly like to take into account the
popular tradition of the peoples of Latin America. Although
they apparently submit to the dogmatics of officialdom, they live
their own dogmatics which is not very developed in terms of
rational concepts. What we are saying is not new. It is an old
tradition among subjugated peoples to utilize for their own lives
what they believe worthwhile in the culture or religion of the
subjugators; the poor then encourage those holding power to
believe that they are dancing to their tune, and that they believe
in their "saints." That being the case, we can say that the poor
generally acknowledge the importance of Jesus; they appreciate
him; they are aware of the most important facts about his life;
but they seem to give Mary much more importance. Even though
we know few specifics about her life, she is still the mother, the
sweetness, the one to whom we can run, the one who understands all our afflictions and sufferings, the one who consoles
and protects us.

Mary is the patroness of the various countries of Latin America. Each patroness has a name and her own story which is
intermingled with the history of the people. They are all the face
of Mary, simultaneously a "projection" of the suffering face of
the people and of a yearning for the restoration of life.

In their own "dogmatics" the people have the greatest intimacy with Mary. One can entrust secrets to her; she can hear
them and keep them in her heart. She walks with the poor "over
hard roads full of rock and sand"; she understands women's
secrets, even the most intimate, and nothing scandalizes her.
The same is not true of Jesus, at least with the same intensity.
From this angle the figure of Jesus is less rooted in the people.

This is partly due to various historical circumstances and also to an underlying reality, whose roots are anthropologico-cultural and psychological.

With the recognition of Christianity by the Roman Empire starting with Constantine (fourth century), the figure of Jesus was partly assimilated to that of the emperor. Documents and especially paintings from that period of history attest to this assimilation. Jesus came to be clothed in the garments of the Roman emperor and the apostles stood by his side like consuls. This was the beginning of a distancing from the people. The figure of Jesus stood closer to those who hold power in this world, and hence further from the masses.

This figure underwent changes in subsequent periods of history, especially in the West. For example, there was an emphasis on the Lord of sorrows, so popular among Latin Americans, evoking pity, and to some extent, a source of explanation and consolation for the various sufferings of the poor. In the bloody crucified one, the impoverished people see their cross and their own blood spilt, although they do not express this clearly but rather through their own religious language, which is rich in symbolic expressions. Other images of Jesus followed: Christ the king, the sacred heart of Jesus, and so on. Still, none of these images/devotions, despite their popularity, especially in certain places, is the predominant devotion throughout Latin America.

We do not think this is the place to trace out the history of how the different images of Jesus have succeeded one another and the various places where they are most venerated. That is not our purpose. The references we have made to them serve only to situate better the question of the relationship with Mary which we are now considering.

From an anthropological and psychological viewpoint, the figure of Jesus sometimes merges into the figure of *God,* and sometimes into that of the *Son* of the Father. Therefore with Jesus comes a relationship of children to the father or one in which the Son of God is viewed almost as a brother.

Because of the historical and cultural experience of our Latin American peoples, the relationship with father figures is quite problematic due to the absence of the real father from the family or the cruelty of father figures in our *macho* and patriarchal cultures. The father has little involvement with matters of family intimacy and feeling, since very often he is hardly ever at home.

The figure of the brother is not very defined. At first glance the sibling is someone with whom one competes, especially for family love. Despite the affection we may have for him (or her) we cannot always open our heart to the extent that this relationship could become a projected ideal in which we might seek affection and consolation. The brother or sister is my equal, as lacking as I am. We need someone "different" to make up for certain deficiencies that are part of our being.

All this shows us the complex presence of elements of a psychological and cultural nature conditioning the different expressions of popular religion.

It is Mary's maternal side that the people especially prize. That is also true of the institutional tradition of the Christian churches. Motherhood brings Mary close to the people. In saying that, we do not mean to say that maternal qualities are found only in women, as though only they were capable of taking care of children with love. Some men, both young and old, also have this ability to "mother" children, to show them affection, rock them to sleep, protect them. We do not think this is the problem. The whole matter revolves around what a particular figure represents for a social group. The symbolic dimension of human life can help us a great deal in understanding what happens in the deepest human relations.

The word "symbol" should not be understood as designating something unreal, or something figurative, or something that merely represents another thing. A symbol is something real, something that is an integral part of the human being, something that can sum up a feeling and demand an interpretation. Only human beings can express themselves symbolically, that is, only they can "build" symbols to express what goes beyond them and express with symbols what mere speech cannot accomplish.[35]

Symbols have an inexhaustible meaning. There is always room for something more in them. Therefore, it may be said that they have an inconceivable wealth of meanings and that they are an expression of the mysterious human reality that always intends to say more than the words used to express it.

The mother is not just the one engendering, she who has

given birth to a child. The mother is an all-embracing symbol that almost always sends out positive energy, affection, warmth, understanding, life. We are not pointing here to a particular mother, but rather to the symbolic figure of the Mother, and her "function" in society, and especially her function in the religious world of the poor of Latin America. This great maternal symbol has a name: *Mary.*

All this partly explains the primacy the poor give to Mary, and it demands that we all make a more respectful effort to understand better the vital needs concealed in the pursuit of their mother Mary. In seeking out their mother people are to some extent seeking the protection they enjoyed at the very beginning of life. That beginning is the moment of most complete intimacy when one's being seems completely protected by a superior being. This return to one's beginnings is repeated very often in human existence, and especially in religious structures, which in an ideal fashion rebuild human life on the basis of a new family; this is a family in which people have close emotional and social relationships with beings endowed with extraordinary qualities.

The insatiable human desire for happiness is expressed in religious language; that desire idealizes personal figures, including the father and the mother; it creates utopias and constantly nourishes new experiences.

Mary is the mother, the ideal mother, the mother of our dreams, even when we want to make her like any other Mary. She continues to be the most beautiful, the most understanding, the kindest, the most affectionate. Our effort to make her equal betrays our desire that she continue to exist as different.

The purpose of our present reflection, which is of a rather anthropological nature, is briefly to introduce the question of the people's dogmatics as related to the dogmatics established by the church institution.

In the dogmatics of the Latin American people there is a series of elements that fit with institutional dogmatics, despite the different shading of the latter, presented with the formality and style that typify ecclesiastical documents. In the former, it is the aspects of life that are brought to the fore, while in the latter the most important thing seems to be statements made supporting one position or attacking another.

What is important for the people is saving life—their own individual, collective, and cultural life. What is important is saving their right to exist with at least a minimum of dignity. Hence dogmatic details laid down from within another cultural world do not count for much. Even the separating of Marian dogmas—so that one is about Mary's virginity, another about her as Mother of God, another about the immaculate conception, and one about the assumption—is important for the people only to the extent that each dogma is absorbed into the effort of life and death they experience at the extremes of their history.

Life is such a tough battle that the relationship with Mary, she who is "alive in God," full of affection and power, is direct: it is connected to the people's immediate and vital needs, since the life of the poor unfolds basically at this level. Mary has to do with children crying because they are hungry, with giving birth, with the lack of work, with a harvest that has not produced much, with one's husband leaving, with sickness, with homelessness and so many other problems in daily life. She is the relief people are longing for when they cry, "Help me, dear mother of sorrows."

This is when the urgent yearning of the poor changes Mary's "face-of-the-people" into a "face-for-the-people." Mary is then the "saint," the "mother," "my mother in heaven," the person who is "for the people." People direct their unsatisfied desires, requests, fears, and uncertainties toward her. At this level of human and religious experience she is more an individual person than a collective/people whom I address. It is one's individual "self" that must speak to her of one's problems, complain to her, and ask for the graces one needs. Nevertheless, despite this personal aspect she continues to exist beyond the personal, since many people can address her simultaneously. Such a relationship with Mary puts us on another level of existence that does not completely mix with institutional dogmatics, rather like what happens with oil and water. There are two realities here, two different cultural worlds: one holds sway through the power of carefully prepared discourse while the other asserts itself through the force of numbers and the existential need of those who compose it.

It is in this sense that we can say that the formulation of institutional dogmatics is "not much of a problem" for the poor, since it is not very well understood, and ultimately the poor transform it to serve their own situation in history.

This is not the same as saying that one need not know institutional dogmatics or that it has no value within the church's tradition. We are dealing with another problem here, that of the gulf between where the poor live, because of their own situation, and the dogmatic discussions and their official formulations. Hence, in order to place ourselves at the service of the Kingdom of Life, we must turn our eyes and our senses to the religious experience of the poor, of the people who cannot deal with the words and argumentation, but are fully involved in life and in the struggle to survive.

When it comes to experiencing faith in Mary, the people are way ahead of any theological endeavors. Their experience is primary, and it is what generates subsequent reflection and the new formulations emerging from that reflection.

CHAPTER V

Some Traditions of Devotion to Mary in Latin America

Conquerors and conquered, owners and workers, religious and lay people have experienced their relationship with Mary over the centuries-long history of Christian faith in Latin America. Impelled by its own interests, each group has claimed Mary for its own, and so she has taken part in the conflicts of life and death, victory and defeat of different groups within the complex Latin American social fabric. Our primary aim in this chapter is not to make either a personal or a historic judgment about the different relationships with Mary, but rather to try to draw out aspects of this devotion in order to demonstrate the diversity of our social reality and the complexity of the question of the relationship between those who "live in history" and those who "live in God."

Any view of the religious dimension of human existence must take account not only of its ideological component and fidelity to institutional dogma, but also of the experience that springs from the depths of human beings who reach out for something to hold on to, beyond the frightful and menacing limits of their immediate history. This behavior seems to be a kind of anthropological necessity, something we cannot run away from if we are actually to glimpse something of the human mystery.

1. THE COLONIAL PERIOD

Mary was regarded as the great protector of the conquistadors. That experience went hand-in-hand with the economic interests of the Spanish and Portuguese crowns, since drawing the Indians to the Christian faith was part of what the conquest was about. Increasing the number of Christians meant increasing the number of the king's subjects. All these elements were interconnected in the view of sixteenth-century Christendom.

The language of the conquest clearly demonstrates the warlike and combative nature of Iberian Catholicism, which was viewed by its practitioners as the only way to salvation for humankind. Hence to pull Indians away from the perdition to which their idols were inexorably leading them, and to show them the light of the cross and the affection of the Virgin meant saving their souls and leading them to eternal happiness. This enterprise of "salvation" was as important as conquering new lands for the glory of the Spanish and Portuguese crowns.

The enterprise of the conquest was so vast and so daring that it was not enough to have the protection and backing of the Catholic monarchs and the pope. The conquest was regarded as the work of the Virgin, the powerful and yet tender lady, who was concerned about protecting the Spanish and Portuguese believers and converting the Indians to faith in her divine Son. So it was customary to say, as did Fray Antonio María, "No one can doubt that the conquest was successful because of the Queen of the Angels!"[1]

During the first generation of the conquest there was a great deal of religious violence, and the indigenous religious culture was destroyed in the name of the purity and truth of Christianity. The conquerors believed that the Indians' gods were evil and that they would most certainly lead them to hell. Since heaven was more important than earth, any means could be used to ensure the happiness that would follow this passing ephemeral life. So, at the outset of the conquest of Mexico, for example, the conquerors sternly warned the Indians "to remove the idols from that house . . . for they would lead their souls to hell. There was an attempt to make them understand other holy and good

things, and to convince them to replace their idol with an image of Our Lady and a cross that Hernán Cortés had given
them. . . ."²

Another significant example is the action of Don Pedro Al-
varado, who conquered Guatemala. After defeating the Indians
at Utatlán, where many lost their lives, he thanked the heavens
for his victory by means of a great feast in honor of the Virgin.
On that occasion, after Mass, Fray Bartolomeo de Olmedo
"preached, and there were many Indians present and he told
them many things about our faith, he spoke good theologies to
them, which they say the friar knew, and it pleased God that
more than thirty Indians wanted to be baptized and the friar
baptized them two days later, and others wanted to be baptized. . . ."³

The conquerors always saw Mary as on their side and against
the Indians whom they regarded as infidels. Theirs was a holy
war and so the Virgin protected them in their harsh efforts to
bring the Indians to the faith.

It is said—and this is certainly a product of Spanish Christian
ideology—that in Cuzco (Peru), during a violent battle between
Indians and Spaniards, at a place known as Sunturhuari, a Que-
chua name, the Virgin Mary came to the aid of the Spaniards
when the Indians had them surrounded. It was nighttime and
the Indians were armed and seeking revenge when suddenly

> there appeared in the air Our Lady with the Child Jesus
> in her arms, with magnificent radiance and beauty, and she
> stood before them. The infidels, gazing at that wonder,
> were amazed. They felt a dust like sand falling into their
> eyes and hence they could not see any more and did not
> know where they were. They had to turn around and go
> home before the Spaniards could come out and do battle
> with them.⁴

The Spaniards considered themselves faithful servants of
Mary. Any methods used against the "infidels" seemed not only
approved by Mary, but were even the work of the Virgin. She
was credited with bringing about all manner of situations and
using all manner of means to save the Indians, since what was

at stake was the expansion of her Son's Kingdom.

Despite their power, the conquistadors thought they were "weak" vis-à-vis the Indians, and yet "strong" in the power of the Christian faith for which they battled the infidels to the death. Again, this behavior is part of the insidious ideological structure of the warrior Catholicism of the conquerors, as though theirs were a "holy war."[5]

With the second generation of the conquest, veneration of Mary began to become an integral part of the customs of Spanish and Portuguese America. After the annihilation of countless thousands of "infidels" and the resulting victory of the conquerors over the natives, there began a process in which the conquered adapted to the new dominant religious culture. No doubt the worship of the mother-goddess, common to the indigenous peoples, as well as the worship of other deities, merged with elements brought along with the conquistadors' faith. In the prologue to the first edition of his study of veneration of the Virgin (see n. 1 of chap. IV), Rubén Ugarte speaks about the moralizing and civilizing influence of veneration of Mary:

> Mary is an idea so sublime and yet so much in tune with our being that loving her and devotion to her cannot but awaken feelings of sensitivity and nobility and the highest aspirations even in the most uncultivated hearts, disposing the soul for the exercise of virtue. . . . This ideal of the Virgin was able to attract the attention of the poor inhabitants of our most remote regions. . . . It inspired them with an affection that softened their customs, that made their labors less harsh, and even made their isolation less lonely. Mary even influenced their art, so that with their rustic instruments they addressed to her the sweetest sounds, and their rough hands shaped stone and wood and erected carvings in granite and cedar that today amaze those who visit her shrines.

The integration of devotion to Mary did not take place immediately or easily. Those evangelizing at that time were always preoccupied with replacing the deity of the mother-goddess with Our Lady in order to prevent, as they saw it, the continuation of idolatry. Judgment of what constituted idolatry was, of course, made on the basis of the criteria of the Christianity of the conquerors, especially the missionaries. Due to their own limitations in language, culture, and education, and because they thought they were the unique possessors of the truth, they were unable to grasp the depth of the Indians' spirituality.[6] Nevertheless, one can say that after a time there was a syncretist integration of the great deities of the Indians (and later of blacks) into Christianity. A typical example of this integration is the shrine on Mount Tepeyac in Mexico, which was the destination of pilgrimages to the goddess Tonantzin-Cihuacóatl and later to Our Lady of Guadalupe.[7]

This process of integration is rather similar to the procedure of early Christianity, where the practice was to Christianize pagan customs and temples and then use them. The process of evangelization in Latin America followed the same principle. The constitutions of the First Council of Lima in 1552 read: ". . . We order that all idols and places of adoration that might exist in the villages where there are Christian Indians be burned and destroyed, and if the place is suitable, a church should be built there or at least a cross should be erected."[8] It was undoubtedly the missionaries' intention to eliminate the traces of primitive Indian religion as far as possible in order to achieve a religious and political integration that was more in harmony with the hegemony of Christianity and the dominant political power.

As part of this integration a number of confraternities dedicated to the Virgin Mary were set up in Spanish and Portuguese America. It is important to note that these confraternities maintained the division into social groups characteristic of that period. There were confraternities for Indians, for blacks, and for whites, each with its own special feast days, processions, and works of charity for the poorest. The Dominicans and the Jesuits in particular promoted these confraternities, although later they took on a decidedly lay character. In many places throughout Latin America these confraternities still exist and they maintain many of their ancient traditions.

2. THE ERA OF COLONIAL INDEPENDENCE

During the period of the wars of independence from Spain (nineteenth century), the role of the Blessed Virgin Mary [*María*

Santísima] was as important as it was during the colonization period. The leaders of the independence struggle of the Latin American countries believed that their devotion to Mary was one of the most powerful weapons for winning autonomy for their countries.

Together with the "liberators," clergy and religious supported the cause of their countries in the name of faith and called on the people to do the same. The institutional church was allied with the native oligarchies. Defending their country and their religion constituted a single movement.[9] For example, at the meeting of notables in Trujillo (Peru) to take the oath of independence, Don Manuel Tadeo Fernández de Córdoba asked the notables to "swear with him to God Our Lord with a sign of the cross, to defend to the very last drop of blood the Roman Catholic and apostolic religion, the purity of Mary Most Holy, Our Lady, from the first instant of her Immaculate Conception, and our country." All gave their assent.[10]

José de San Martín appointed the Virgin of Mount Carmel as "general" over his armies. After victories in Cacabuco and Maipú he sent his staff to the Virgin of Mount Carmel at the Franciscan house in Mendoza; the purpose of sending them was to honor her who had been and continued to be the high commander of the army of the Andes.

In Mexico Hidalgo cultivated the same devotion to Mary. An image of Our Lady of Guadalupe painted on cloth was hoisted on a spear and carried at the head of his army until the victory of Celaya. His successor Morelos maintained this same devotion along with his troops. Iturbide, who consolidated Mexico's independence, established the Order of Our Lady of Guadalupe to reward all those who had given outstanding service to the country.

It is also well known that Simón Bolívar was devoted to Our Lady of Belén [Bethlehem]. The story is told that in one battle with a stronger enemy, Bolívar raised the image of the Virgin he carried with him and prayed to her for protection. The enemy fled and, safe once more, Bolívar paid homage to the Virgin.

In Ecuador it was the same Virgin under the title of Our Lady of Mercy who helped the patriots from the time they issued the first cry of rebellion until the moment when independence was consolidated in 1823.

Although the liberators of Spanish America were typically very devoted to the Virgin Mary, the same was not true in Portuguese America. This does not mean that there was less devotion to Mary in Brazil, for besides the fact that such devotion was very popular, starting in colonial times when shrines and chapels of various kinds were built in her honor, Mary was also the protectress of various liberation movements, including those of slaves.[11] However, the question here is that of liberation struggles, and it is on this point that there is a significant difference between Brazil and Spanish America.

Brazil's independence process was influenced by Freemasonry and the French Enlightenment, and it was conceived and carried out by intellectuals among whom a certain anti-clericalism prevailed. We need only remind ourselves that the independence of Brazil was "proclaimed" by Don Pedro I, first emperor of Brazil. The very person who wielded Portuguese power separated Brazil from Portugal. This seemed to be a move for independence, but actually it was a move to preserve the political and economic power of the Brazilian elites from Portugal and especially from England, the power then ascendant economically.

It is known that Don Pedro I was a Catholic Mason and that he always placed the interests of the Brazilian crown above the needs of Roman Catholicism, which at that point in Brazil was beginning to feel the consequences of incipient Ultramontanism (centralization of Roman power at the expense of the autonomy of local churches).

From a "legal" standpoint, Brazil was a Catholic country as was established in article 5 of the 1824 Imperial Constitution. However, in the "real country" there existed a religious syncretism seemingly under the official structure of national Catholicism.[12] The people had a vast number of devotions, some of them especially connected to the Virgin. Nevertheless, such devotions do not seem to have played a decisive role in the movement for independence, although they were undeniably present.

In this respect the written history of Brazil[13] does not provide us with information that would enable us to discern the political power of Marian devotion during Brazil's independence struggles. We can only surmise that devotion to Mary was always present in the popular strata and that it sustained them in their impoverished and difficult daily effort, far from palace decisions and great power plays.

3. FROM THE ESTABLISHMENT OF NATIONAL OLIGARCHIES TO THE PRESENT

As we have seen, devotion to Mary retains an anthropological and ideological substrate common to all adherents, which is expressed in the pursuit of their needs and in the defense of their interests. This meant that after political independence was achieved in the various Latin American countries, Marian devotion developed in different directions, varying according to who the adherents were and who "organized" and/or "owned" the development of a particular devotion.

We do not intend to attempt a history of the development of Marian devotions during the nineteenth and twentieth centuries, but simply to recall the prominent place they occupied, especially among the poorest.[14]

Marian devotions proliferated during the eighteenth, nineteenth, and early twentieth centuries with the growing presence and extension of European religious congregations, each of which implanted devotion to the Virgin of its own birthplace. Indeed, this process dates from the colonial period and accelerated during the following centuries.

Just as they did during the struggles for political independence, subsequent rulers continued to "consecrate" the various countries to the Virgin in alliance with the religious authorities of each period. This religious legitimation accorded well with the various kinds of Latin American populism in their striving to win over the masses. There were exceptions to this kind of behavior, but they are insignificant in the overall picture. The "new caudillos," whether civil or military, generally expressed their devotion in order to be seen to do so by the people and thereby win votes or acclaim. In this way they made use of Mary's image to serve their own individual interests.

Nevertheless, Mary has been the mother and great companion for many of the people's struggles in Latin America. Many peasant movements in Brazil, Bolivia, and Peru have been stimulated by the people's love for the Virgin who struggles with them for their liberation. Another important example is devotion to La Purísima (Immaculate Conception) in Nicaragua when the Sandinistas were struggling against the Somoza regime. This was obviously an expression of the people's faith and attachment to Mary, and in many parts of Nicaragua the devotion gave the people strength.[15] In El Salvador the same love of the people for Mary led Archbishop Oscar Romero to say, "the true homage a Christian can pay the Virgin is, like her, to make the effort to incarnate the life of God in the trials of our transitory history."[16] This incarnation has taken place in many places throughout Latin America, inviting us once again to take a fresh look at traditional Mariology to discern a Marian theology, the fruit of this new phase in the history of Christian faith.

4. APPEARANCES, CURES, AND MIRACLES

No sooner had he said this than he was lifted up before their eyes in a cloud which took him from their sight. They were still gazing up into the heavens when two men dressed in white stood beside them. "Men of Galilee," they said, "why do you stand here looking up at the skies? This Jesus who has been taken from you will return, just as you saw him go up into the heavens" (Acts 1:9–11).

After sunset, as evening drew on, they brought him all who were ill, and those possessed by demons. Before long the whole town was gathered outside the door. Those whom he cured, who were variously afflicted, were many, and so were the demons he expelled. But he would not permit the demons to speak, because they knew him (Mark 1:32–4).

These New Testament texts undoubtedly go back to Jesus. Early tradition has left us a number of testimonies about him that have been made permanent in the New Testament writings, attesting to cures, miracles, and appearances after his resurrection. Absolutely nothing is said about his mother, Mary, in this regard—absolute silence, like the silence surrounding the lives of countless thousands who have anonymously paved the way for the signs of God's Kingdom.

If scripture does not say anything about Mary's miracles, cures, and appearances, the subsequent history of Christians has produced many pages about them, and throughout that history Christians have experienced many signs from Mary similar to those that her son performed during his life. It is said that one day Mary went into a deep sleep, and as happened at the birth of her son there came many angels singing *"gloria"* and they drew her up to the bosom of the One who had created the new hope for humankind in her.

She has appeared and appears in many ways, many times, and in different places. She has talked with very simple people, done favors, and consoled many people.

Hope does not die. It is the sister of human yearning. Both are part of our deepest roots. Hence even when she has gone to "sleep," Mary awakens, gives new inspiration, offers help in working through problems, and sinks once more into the sleep of life, indicating that she is always present even though she often seems to be absent or in a "very deep sleep." Mary is "alive in God," and therefore she lives especially in the historic hope of believing peoples.

Today more than in other periods we are discovering that Christians have claimed for Mary almost everything said about the activity of Jesus. She also performs the signs of the Kingdom, transcending the historic time of her mortal existence. Blind people see, paralytics walk, lepers are cured, peoples rise out of slavery, and in these ways signs of God's justice become manifest in the complex fabric of human history.

It is not our purpose to describe Mary's miracles and appearances throughout the history of the peoples of Latin America. There are specialized works describing the history of the appearances and miracles of the Virgin in various locations.[17] Our aim is specifically theological, that is, we want to try to express, through the poverty of words, the anthropological and theological significance of the breakthrough of the extraordinary—appearance, cure, miracle—especially in the life of the poor, of those who go to the Virgin as a last resort in their harsh existence. We also want to show a similarity between the way the poor relate to Mary and the way they relate to all those who "live in God" and who enjoy certain privileges or special powers for the sake of those who "live in history."

To begin with, it is worth noting that Mary's cures are always described as taking place in the context of an extreme situation with no way out. The evil affecting the person is dangerous and is leading him or her to death, whether immediately or gradually. In almost all shrines and places of pilgrimage dedicated to the Virgin, the room for votive offerings is the symbolic expression of humankind's sufferings and martyrdoms. Photos, crutches, clothing, parts of the human body carved out of wood or wax, manacles, chains, and other objects are symbols of the restoration of life obtained through the influence of the Virgin.[18] They also indict the presence of the "moral evil" that was afflicting each worshiper. In that room the object serves to name the evil and at the same time represents the evil eliminated. To say the evil in words or symbolically through objects is a way of exorcising it, of trying to expel it for good. It is a specific evil, one that has an exact name. It is not something generic or abstract but that which was preventing a full life.[19]

Mary combats the evil affecting those who believe and thus restores life. To restore life and deliver from evil are traits that make Mary's power a divine power. This is not expressed in words. This is something lived within a religious experience that is almost inaccessible on the level of words. One need only look at the places of pilgrimage dedicated to the Virgin and see those who have received favors from her, their faces showing the deep emotion they feel. Here we are very close to the mystery that constitutes and transcends us. Reason alone cannot grasp the element of "wonder" in a cure, a re-encounter, the attaining of grace. We must go further, to where the poor and humble know how to go almost spontaneously since their vital powers have not been almost totally dominated by cool reason that dissects facts, breaks up their unity, uses them in a laboratory, and finds their causes and component elements. The element of "wonder" eludes this kind of analysis. Even if we describe it, we cannot possess it. The element of wonder is not of the same order as science, but is rather of the order of poetry, of the poetry of life, where another language holds sway and where all senses must be alert in order to grasp something of the enchantment that is spread around.

The wonderful, miracles, and cures take place in the order of human materiality or bodiliness. Their effects are palpable and can be seen and checked in everyday life. So we can say that miracles validate the human, bring lost human beings to find themselves once more, restored to life in their personal and social history. What Mary does in the the realm of the wonderful brings about "rebirth." Something new takes place – as though in this newness the supplicants were once more begotten within her, now freed of the evil previously tormenting them.

In this relationship there takes place what is commonly called the "experience of God," the experience of the divine Absolute working within the limits of the human. This is one variation of the experience of the mystics, who feel God in their flesh, in their whole being and who manage to express this treasure poetically.[20] Through the miracles of Mary and of others who "live in God," the poor undergo a different mystical experience, one that does not follow official patterns and is not sanctioned by officialdom, but one – in our view – every bit as rich. They also live that experience in their body; they are caught up in "ecstasy" at the moment of the cure or by the power of their internal dialogue with the "saint." God "speaks to us in many ways," and this multiplicity of ways expresses the multiplicity of languages and expressions that constitute us.

Appearances express the power of the yearning for the divine in humans – a divine that men, women, and children can see and grasp with their senses – and prove its existence and action. Despite its apparent absence, its sometimes unbearable silence, the divine is there. Scientific reason cannot prove it. Rather the divine is grasped by mystical reason and the senses that can speak of appearances and direct dialogues with the divine.

Those "favored" with appearances of the Virgin are relatively few in number compared to those "favored" with cures or other miracles. When the Virgin appears she always insists on one or more points connected with the moment in history and with the formation of the person favored. We believe that, from a religious viewpoint, the messages she seems to impart are less important than the circumstances of the appearances themselves. To begin with, it is interesting that the Virgin always appears in a Catholic setting: she has already taken a position on the religious controversies of past ages. Secondly, the "appearance" must be approved by the institutional church through long years of investigating and questioning those "favored." Only after the appearance is declared to be true is public worship permitted. The intention of the Catholic church is to avoid having Mary's countenance disfigured with false images, which often have a purely subjective stamp.[21]

Thirdly, in appearances the Virgin generally assumes positions that are clearly ideological. She often, for instance, seeks to save the people from communism or socialism; she points out the dangers of modern society, and recommends prayer, fasting, and penance. In this respect the appearances at Lourdes and Fatima, and lately in Medjugorje (Yugoslavia) are typical examples. Recently that part of the Nicaraguan church that is anti-Sandinista has exploited devotion to the Virgin in order to combat the regime that has been in power since 1979.[22]

It does not seem useful to us at this point to discuss the procedure of the Catholic church on the three points we have just listed. We only intend to raise some suspicions about possible manipulation of devotion to the Virgin. Our specific aim is to reflect on the different expressions of the people's faith, to try to find their meaning, while remaining quite aware that the question we are approaching is complex.[23]

Our observations are based on our own experiences in meeting believers. This means we are putting forward hypotheses and, in our opinion, hypotheses are all that can be proposed in this field of religious symbols. In this connection we adopt the thought of Rubem Alves when he refers to religious discourse as poetic discourse: "The fact is that poetic discourse does not seek to be truth. To seek to be truth is to be content with simply being word, a weak thing, a thing that dwells in reason. . . ."[24]

The appearance is a religious word, a poetic word, because it is something that goes beyond what can be proven; it is human reality transcending the limits of humanity. What is most important in the appearance is the sensible, physical connection between the world of those who "live in history" and the world of those who "live in God." There is a dialogue we yearn for in the depths of being that for brief instants becomes possible, as though at this moment heaven and earth merged, life and death were joined, the living and the dead spoke the same language. It is an instant of wonder that the scriptures have described and many biblical figures have experienced. It is "seeing the divine," "conversing with the divine," "hearing the divine" as if this experience entailed a deep "plunge" of human beings into their own roots.[25] This "plunge" casts a spell on the person, who then goes forth to proclaim what he or she has "seen." But the telling of what has been "seen" is no longer the experience but simply a narration. Nevertheless, it still has power and touches others and these others also want to experience the "invisible," to plunge into the roots of their being, even if they do not formulate their experience exactly in this manner. Those who hear but do not see are also blessed. They converse with the deity in their hearts, and the divinity hears them. They experience the divinity in their own way, within their own limits. Hence the expressions "I have spoken to Our Lady," "She has looked at me," "She has heard me," "She has given me peace," "She has cured my pains," reveal a total experience of being, a mystical experience, the religious expression of a people seeking life.

As the popular poet puts it:

> I'm a bumbling country bumpkin,
> Our Lady of Aparecida,
> Because I don't know how to pray
> I only wanted to show my face. . . .

An appearance is an interlude in men's and women's ordinary experience, which they are left abandoned to suffer alone. In an appearance the chalice of life is drained to the bottom, but now life is less lonely, as though it were really unfolding under the gaze of One who listens to me and desires my welfare. The appearance makes the struggle for existence more bearable. The heavens become our allies and the burden we must carry seems lighter. Thus, one often hears among the poor, "Put this in the hands of Mary Immaculate," "Stick with Our Lady, she is going to help you out." When Mary comes into the picture she brings a possible solution; she brings in other people, if only the neighbor to whom one describes the problem. Certainly this kind of relationship can be experienced with other saints, and with Jesus, but since our reflection here is basically Mariological, we are most interested in learning more about our relationship with Mary.

Another important aspect that should be emphasized is the fact that Mary is a woman. The appearance is of a woman, a woman's body recognized as such, and one that consequently brings about a relationship that is different from the relationship with a person of male gender. In the mystical tradition, women's relationship with Jesus is deep down always openly or latently erotic, the expression of a total love, of an unconditioned surrender to the beloved One.[26]

We understand the word "erotic" in a positive way, as meaning the thrust of all energy of love toward the one loved. Hence it entails not only so called "spiritual" energies, but all bodily energy as centered on the love relationship. With regard to Mary, the erotic dimension is more diffuse, although very beautiful love poems have been dedicated to her.[27] What is most salient with regard to Mary is a seeking after the Mother, the symbolism of maternity that seems to be something deeply basic and primeval in the human being. The "womb" is where we first exist. Hence, certain expressions from popular hymns—for instance, "Mother sweet and kind," "Hide me deep within your face"—express well what we are trying to say, and there are many other examples along the same lines that express affection and the need for protection.

In this respect, iconography is also very significant. There are pictures and statues in which Mary appears with a huge mantle draped over a vast number of people. Her body is large, bigger than all the others. She stands out as the "Great Mother," protecting and defending her offspring, comprised of young people, old men, old women, adults, and children. Near her, they are obviously safe, protected, free of the threats and dangers of everyday life. Such paintings and sculptures express well the frailty of the human condition, and people's search for security and kindness, while also expressing symbolically Mary's power.

In the expression of Mary's power is concealed the yearning to be strong, which is characteristic of human beings when they are confronted with their frailty. Such iconography represents "Mary, Mother of People" (also called Mother of Mercy), a devotion originally from Europe that is especially widespread in some areas of Northern and Northeastern Brazil. Another kind of picture and sculpture common in Northeast Brazil is the image of "the Child Mary," which shows Mary learning the scriptures, which Saint Anne, her mother, is teaching her. It is important to realize that in popular circles there is a tradition of a feminist handing on of the faith, a tradition that needs to be reactivated and retrieved today, especially in the practice of Christian base communities where women unquestionably play a leadership role.

Relationship with Mary is also relationship to woman as source of life. So poems addressed to Mary often stress, besides motherhood, the aspect of a connection to nature. That perspective is present in Revelation where a woman (whom tradition later came to understand as Mary) is "clothed with the sun, with the moon under her feet, and on her head [is] a crown of twelve stars."[28] Under the inspiration of Revelation, especially in the seventeenth century, popular piety has dressed Mary with the sun, put the moon under her feet, embroidered her mantle with stars, and has spoken of her as "sweet honeycomb," and as fruitful plant, light of the dawn, star of the sea, lily most pure, rose without thorns, beautiful dove. Mary unites all of nature within herself as though she were a kind of quintessence of the universe.

So in litanies to the Virgin, especially from the sixteenth century, Mary embodies in herself a synthesis of creation and of the great moments of the history of Israel and of nature:

> Hail Mary, Daughter of God the Father,
> Hail Mary, Mother of God the Son,
> Hail Mary, Spouse of the Holy Spirit,
> Hail Mary, Temple of the Trinity. . . .
>
> Mother most pure,
> Virgin most faithful, . . .

Throne of Solomon,
Glory of Jerusalem,
Morning light.[29]

Relationship with Mary is complex, uniting the elements of nature, eroticism, and the people's traditional faith, although one element or another will be emphasized depending on time, place, and the people involved.

Mary's appearances, cures, and miracles in Latin America are numbered in the thousands in her countless shrines and more than 150 titles—Our Lady of Grace, of Lourdes, of the Rosary, of Aparecida, of Conception, Virgin Most Pure, of Good Childbirth, of Good Death, of Liberation . . .[30] It is impossible to count all the stories, all the origins of devotions, all the miracles. Stories about Mary are intermingled with the life of the people, forming a single cloth where the real and the imaginary mesh together and where yesterday and today open out to tomorrow.

Let us take a closer look at the history of the Virgin who is proclaimed patroness of our continent, Our Lady of Guadalupe. Her story will serve as a small example to stimulate our thinking so we may understand other stories of Mary. We will also devote a few lines to the Virgin of Conceição Aparecida, patroness of Brazil, and as we conclude this chapter, we will briefly indicate other Latin American Marian devotions.

5. THE APPEARANCE OF OUR LADY OF GUADALUPE

Of all the devotions to the Virgin Mary in Latin America the only one that can be called the fruit of a properly supernatural[31] appearance is that of Guadalupe. Elsewhere in Latin America devotions to the Virgin have sprung from an image either found or carved by natives or brought by missionaries. Guadalupe therefore occupies a privileged place in Latin American Mariology, for it means basically that the Virgin adopts the "natives" of Mexico as their mother and with them adopts the Latin American people as a whole.

The story of this appearance and the historical circumstances that make up the backdrop against which it took place reveal the integration of Mary, whose appearances belong to another cultural world, into the indigenous reality of Latin America.

The "little Indian woman" and later the *morenita* ["little dark woman"], as she was called, are expressions that come from the Indians' assimilation of the European "deities," an assimilation based on their traditional devotions, which were transformed by the religious "newness" brought by the conquerors.

We do not intend to present and analyze the many aspects of the appearance of the Virgin of Guadalupe. For that purpose there are many works both old and contemporary[32] that deal with the question. Some even utilize knowledge of Náhuatl, the language in which the testimony of Juan Diego was first transcribed. Our aim is to recollect the depth of the religious experience that took place at Guadalupe and to illustrate our earlier theological reflection on the Virgin's appearances.

We are simply making an effort to enter into the description of the appearance and to view it as a religious experience that reveals a deep dimension of the human. We will not analyze the differences between translations of the account or questions of historical criticism connected to the text, nor even the divergent interpretations of the dialogue between the Indian and the Virgin. We leave this difficult work to specialists in this area.

The Virgin first appeared to the Indian Juan Diego on December 9, 1531, in the village of Cuauhtitlán near Mexico City. The dialogue between the Indian and the Virgin was written down in Náhuatl in 1533 by an Indian named Antonio Valeriano, who studied with the Jesuits at Tlatelolco. This transcript was translated from Náhuatl by several translators, including Luis Becerra Tanco, from whose Spanish text the following excerpts are translated.[33]

At daybreak, coming to the foot of a small hill which was called Tepeyacac, which means mountain peak, since it stands out from the rest of the mountains surrounding the valley and lake where the city of Mexico lies, and which we today call that of Our Lady of Guadalupe, because of what will be said later on, the Indian heard from the top of the hill and in a row of large rocks lining the plain along the lake, a sweet and beautiful singing which, as he said, sounded to him like a multitude of different birds singing together softly and in harmony, singing back and forth in chorus, in a wonderful concert, whose echoes resounded and were amplified by the high mountain, rising above the little hill; and looking toward the place from which he judged the singing was coming, he saw there a white and shining cloud and around it a beautiful rainbow of different colors coming from the exceedingly bright light in the middle of the cloud. The Indian was enthralled and as though outside himself in a gentle ecstasy, unafraid and unperturbed, feeling in his heart an inexplicable joy and delight, so that he wondered to himself: "What can this be that I am hearing and seeing? Where have I been taken to? Have I perchance been transported to the paradise of delights that our forebearers called the origin of our flesh, garden of flowers, or heavenly land, hidden from the eyes of men?" While he was thus suspended and enraptured, the singing stopped and he heard his name Juan being called by a woman's voice, sweet and delicate, coming from the brightness of that cloud, telling him to come closer. He hurried over to the top of the hill.

In the midst of that brightness he saw a most beautiful Lady, quite similar to the one today visible on her blessed image, according to the indications the Indian gave verbally, before it was copied or anyone else had seen her; he said her garments were shining so brightly that striking the rough boulders rising above the hilltop, it made them seem like carved transparent precious stones and the pine needles and cactus growing there, small and weak in that remoteness, looked like handfuls of fine emeralds, and their branches, trunks, and thorns looked like polished shining gold; and even the soil of a small flat area there seemed like jasper of different colors. And in a gentle and pleasing way that Lady spoke to him in the Mexican language, and said to him: "My son Juan Diego, little and tender one, whom I love with affection, where are you going?" The Indian answered, "I am going, noble mistress and Lady mine, to Mexico City to the district of Tlatelolco to hear the Mass that God's ministers and substitutes put on for us." In response Mary Most Holy said to him, "Be aware, my most beloved son, that I am the ever Virgin Mary, Mother of the true God, author of Life, Creator of all and Lord of heaven and earth, who is everywhere; and it is my desire that a church be built here, where as devout Mother to you and your kind, I will show my loving favor and the compassion I have for the natives and for those who love and seek me, and for those who will seek my protection and call on me in their labors and afflictions; and where I will hear your weeping and prayers to give you consolation and relief; in order that what I want may be accomplished you are to go to Mexico City and to the palace of the bishop who lives there, and you will tell him that I send you and that it is my pleasure that a church be built here for me."

The first thing that strikes the reader of this story is how nature is prepared and "transformed" in the eyes of the "seer" into something marvelous and never before experienced. All nature prepares to accept a great event, a theophany, God's manifestation, or in this case the manifestation of the Mother of God, the Virgin Mary. Birds sing, and their song is soft, harmonious, and enchanting. There breaks forth a rainbow of varied colors, light, a great brightness breaking through the clouds of heaven, leaving the poor Indian in ecstasy. The text recalls the Old Testament theophanies[34] where something happens in nature so that the "Other" may appear and speak to human ears.

Why do human beings describe theophanies in this fashion? What kind of vital experience does this discourse enclose? There seem to be different kinds of theophanies, which nevertheless have points in common. Still, it is noteworthy that a constant is the "extraordinary" element that breaks up the ordinariness of life and interferes with the normal functioning of nature. It is as though the theophany or appearance sought to indicate the need to change something radically. So it uses the extraordinary; it brings together the different forces of nature in order to make it clear through them that something different must happen on the level of human relationships. When the normal words and gestures of life are no longer convincing about the need for change, the "divine" moves into the human heart in order to say what daily experience is already saying, but is not being heeded. The theophany shifts the power of the word to the divinity, thus striving to make the human world sensitive to its own word and to what is happening in its own immediate history.

Theophany is the great poetry of human beings; it is the most advanced use of symbols and sometimes of the prophetic ability to denounce existing evil and to demand that justice be restored. The language of theophany is always analogical. Juan Diego, the Indian, hears a "woman's voice, sweet and delicate," and in the midst of a great "brightness" sees "a most beautiful Lady." The seer sees and hears, asks and responds, but in the midst of intense brightness or in the middle of dense clouds. It is always an encounter with the "Other," with what is not my equal and hence has power and authority to demand that the request be carried out. It is this authority that gives Juan Diego the strength to go to the bishop's palace several times and to suffer more humiliation, to suffer being reminded that he is a poor Indian facing the religious power of the whites, and finally to accomplish his aim.

The theophany contains an ethical demand whose consequences are important, the demand that people actually show absolute respect for others, that they accept, both in principle and in fact, the transcendence of others, respecting the life of others.

The Virgin's insistence that the Indian go to the bishop's house to ask that a chapel be dedicated to her who loves the Indians as beloved sons reflects the conflict between whites and Indians. The "deity" of the whites adopts the Indians, or the Indians adopt that deity as their own in order to assert their right to be respected and be able to live vis-à-vis the power of the whites. There are undoubtedly many interpretations of this event. The gamut is very wide, ranging from the most individualistic interpretation, centered on personal piety, to the recognition of a larger dimension touching on broader social relations among different groups in society—the interpretation we would favor, as seeming better to take into account the conflictive reality experienced in colonial Spanish America.

A second point we want to emphasize is that the divinity, here the Virgin Mary, speaks the Indian's own language. They converse in his language, the language of his people, not that of the colonizer. This fact is quite significant, giving the theophany a very special character. The deity seems to take sides with the weak, with whom it speaks and to whom it manifests itself. It is in order to raise up and strengthen the weak that it uses their language. The Indian understands this and is quite certain of the deity's protection. To speak the same language is to recognize the value of the language being spoken. Here it is the language the colonizer despises, one that had to die so that the one brought from outside, from another world and culture, might live.

The deity takes on the despised language and dispossessed people and uses them to make itself understood. The deity becomes an ally of the Indian collectivity, as oppressed culture. So Guadalupe makes a particular assimilation of Indian and Christian deities. In this connection, reflecting on the transformation of Indian cultures, Jacques Lafaye says, "These shrines are extremely important: they provided the topographical foundation of the syncretism between the great deities of ancient Mexico and Christianity, whose most notable example is that of Mount Tepeyac, the pilgrimage site and shrine of Tonantzin-Cihuacóatl, and later of Our Lady of Guadalupe."[35] Tonantzin the mother-goddess is thus assimilated to the Virgin Mary and goes on to undertake the defense of the Indians as though this were her particular concern.

Tonantzin and subsequently the Virgin Mary come to belong to the Indians, and the Indians become obedient to what the deity wants insofar as they are obedient to the ultimate demand to defend their lives and make the "others," the whites, respect them. Religious cultural assimilation becomes a "weapon" through which the Indians can reassert their worth despite the fact that the presence of the colonizers is a fait accompli.

Obviously, the Indians were not conscious of all these processes when they occurred. They were too involved in the immediate problems of life, where conscious and unconscious are mixed together in the present moment of existence. Such an interpretative hypothesis can only result from a later critical reading, made from a considerable distance in history and after the consequences of these phenomena have been observed. This does not mean, moreover, that one should generalize this observation. It may be valid for the case of Guadalupe and others, but it is not a general rule for all the Virgin's appearances.

In addition, this interpretation is time-specific; that is, it is valid for that particular moment in history and not for the whole subsequent history of the relationship of the Mexican and Latin American peoples to Our Lady of Guadalupe. This means that the relationship with the "saint," or here the Virgin, is subject to a series of historical and sociological conditioning factors. There is no pure "religious experience," that is, one that is purely religious. Human reality is basically a mixture of different aspects of which all are more or less present in everything.

Two further aspects in the text are worthy of note: Mary's expression of motherhood toward the Indian, calling him "my son," and her sending him on a mission.

First, in the land of "mother-goddesses," of female fertility deities in intimate contact with nature, it is not surprising that the aspect of motherhood and everything it entails are bound up with this appearance of Mary and with devotion to Our Lady of Guadalupe. The image of the "new Mother" with traits of the old Indian culture are present in popular culture in a new synthesis.

Second, the mission the Virgin gives the Indian is to build her a church. The initiative for this construction comes from her but the labor actually to accomplish it is to come from the Indian. It is interesting to note that in the New Testament "mission" refers either to Jesus sending his disciples or the Father/God sending Jesus. In this popular Indian tradition it is the woman, Mary, who sends Juan Diego on his mission. For a long time the Indians identified Mary as God, as a female deity, and that prompted the missionaries to fear idolatry and confusion within the incipient Christian faith of the Indians. In this connection Jacques Lafaye says, "It was inevitable that the Indians would regard Guadalupe-Tonantzin, the female image of the universal dual principle, as God."[36] We see this angle of vision as very promising for a feminist reconstruction of popular Christian traditions, a work that must be undertaken courageously in Latin America.[37]

There is one more text of dialogue between Juan Diego and the Virgin that merits inclusion and commentary:

"My little girl, dearest, my Queen and most exalted Lady, I did what you ordered me to do; and although I was not able to get in to see and talk to the bishop for a long time, when I saw him, I gave him your message as you ordered me; he listened to me calmly and with attention but from what I observed in him and in view of the questions he asked me, I gathered that he did not find me trustworthy because he told me to come back again so he could question me more slowly about the purpose of my visit and scrutinize it very closely. He assumed that the church you are asking to be built is my own invention or my own whim and not your will; hence I am requesting that you send for this purpose someone noble and illustrious, worthy of respect, who will compel belief; for you can see, mistress mine, that I am a poor country person, a lowly man of the people, and this affair you are sending me on is not for me; pardon my boldness, O Queen, if in some way I have gone beyond the deference owed to your greatness; far be it from me to have incurred your indignation or displeased you with my response."

Mary Most Holy listened with kindness to what the Indian answered, and after listening to him, replied in this fashion: "Listen, my beloved son, be aware that I have no lack of servants under my command, and they would do what I order; but it is very fitting that you carry out this work, that you request it, and through your participation my will and my desire are to go into effect; so I ask you, my son, and I order you to go back tomorrow to see the bishop and talk to him, and tell him to build for me the church I am asking of you; and the one who sends you is the Virgin Mary, Mother of the True God."[38]

There are several striking elements in this text. The first is the way the Indian treats the Virgin: "My little girl, dearest, O Queen, and most exalted Lady." This kind of address is both affectionate and yet deeply respectful, showing a respect due, as it were, only to deities. Juan Diego's attitude is that of a subject before his queen. It is important to recall that these are the early years of the conquest—the appearance took place in 1531—and these were still years of great conflict and tension between the Indians, and the white conquistadors and all the institutions and culture they brought to the "new world."

Second, we must note the Virgin's insistence that the work she requests of the Indian be carried out. It is the Indian's work or mission that the white man must acknowledge. It is the Indian's word that is at stake, and it is his mission to struggle to be recognized by the whites. In this struggle the Indian is certain that he has absolute backing from the Virgin.

Third, it is quite clear what kind of idea the Indian has of himself: he sees himself as "poor," "wretch," "lowly," "common," an idea formed out of the white men's domination and their values, a domination that has led the Indian to regard as good the "noble" qualities of the colonizer and to fail to appreciate his own despised native culture.

What is striking is that in the Virgin's appearance this state of things seems to be overturned. The Virgin does not have the same problems as the white oppressors. She loves the Indian and adopts him as a son, and this gives him strength to struggle on behalf of her cause before the established church authorities. The task he takes on is daunting but he moves ahead because he cannot refuse the insistent request of his Lady. It is as though carrying out the Virgin's request meant affirming the identity of a people beginning a new phase in its history. This situation reminds us of the courage and vigor with which Old Testament prophets were endowed in their weakness so they could go before kings and princes to denounce Israel's sins and declare the demands of the covenant.[39]

Explicitly the Virgin does not ask for justice; nor does she even lament the Indians' situation. She demands a church where those devoted to her can go and she will lovingly hear their pleas. In such a situation asking for a church seems like very little.

What does this request from the Virgin mean?

We know how much the human psyche reaches for concrete symbols to express its religiosity and to try to express the ineffable. Such behavior is traditional in the religion of all peoples.[40] For example, in early Judaism the ark, and later the temple, were signs of the covenant with the Lord. In Christianity we need only recall how important are the sacred book, and the sacraments, and subsequently the presence of the blessed sacrament.

The temple is always regarded as a different place, a place that marks discontinuity in space in order to introduce sacred space, the place where the deity manifests itself and where one can come into contact with it in a special way.

The Virgin asks the Indian for a "temple." [Spanish and Portuguese *templo* means both "temple" and "church" (building) — trans.] This means she wants to have a dwelling on Indian soil; she wants to be Indian. Thus she becomes a native deity, ready to receive the pleas of the natives and help them in their problems.

Besides this there is one more very important aspect. The presence of the conquerors deprived the Indians not only of their soil but also of their political, social, and religious institutions. They were the conquered, the vanquished, those who had lost the battle. An enormous vacuum opened up in Indian culture. Faith in their deities was in crisis and therefore little by little their ancient deities began to take on the form of the Spaniards' deities. The religious vacuum was thus filled and the power of their gods was restored. (In this regard see, for example, the myth of Quetzalcóatl.)[41] They could call on these gods and they would be heard. These gods granted them a new identity and the confidence they needed to live.

To some extent this process was an instance of the great religious and political principle of the Reformation: *"Cuius regio, illius et religio"* — "The one who holds the region determines the religion." The Americas, once ruled by Indian kings, changed rulers and the new subjects shifted to become adherents of the religion of the "new king" and of those charged with transmitting it.

Hence the appearance of the Virgin of Guadalupe and growing devotion to her had the important role of restoring to an exploited people a religious identity that would help them to build a new national identity. This aspect is very important not only for our understanding of the Indians' devotion to Our Lady of Guadalupe but also for our understanding of some aspects of a conquered people who do not simply allow their culture to die but bring it back to life in other ways so that it will continue to serve them as a source of life and a compass within history.

We are not competent to do a psychological reading of Guadalupe, however interesting that might be. We leave that task to specialists, although we have shared with our readers some of our intuitions in this regard. These may serve as a starting point for reassessing the culture of a people on the basis of their religious devotions. To try to understand the meaning of each devotion, the behavior it prompts both in individuals and in groups, the dialogues that take place with the saint, the hidden yearnings, the devotion's power and limits—this seems to be an important task if we are to help in seeing ourselves as a people with our own identity.

6. OUR LADY OF CONCEIÇÃO APARECIDA: "SAVED" FROM THE WATER TO SAVE THE PEOPLE

Although it is not our purpose to examine the various expressions of devotion to Mary in Latin America but rather to indicate the overall shape of the internal dynamism that governs them, we would like to say a few words about Our Lady Aparecida. She turned black in a river, and was picked up by poor people; she protected slaves, both men and women, was put at the head of confraternities of blacks, and was ultimately proclaimed patroness of Brazil.

Around her there is a popular tradition, according to which she was the object of a "miraculous catch." It is said that in October 1717, while planning for the arrival of the count of Assumar—the governor of the district of São Paulo, who was going to visit Guaratinguetá—the local town council told fishermen to lay in a good supply of fish for the banquets that were to be celebrated.

A fisherman named João Alves and two of his companions

had not caught a single fish near the port of Itaguaçu (Paraíba River). Disappointed with his bad luck, João Alves once more cast the net hoping to catch something. Then, lo and behold, something was caught in the net, and when they drew it up they found in it the body of a Virgin turned black by the water. The head was missing from the statue, and when they threw the net back in they were able to pick it up.[42] After the Virgin had been "saved" from the waters, they caught many fish. That was seen as the first favor the Virgin did for the poor fishermen. Although they wanted the fish they regarded the statue ensnared in their nets as more precious. It marked the beginning of a new phase of life for them, life with the Virgin, the one who had "appeared" [*aparecida*] in the waters.

Scholars quickly proposed hypotheses on the identity of the sculptor. It is most probably the work of a monk in Rio de Janeiro, Frei Agostinho de Jesus. Scholars have also shown that devotion to Our Lady of the Immaculate Conception [*conceição*] was widespread in Portugal and throughout its domains.[43]

It is well known that from the fourteenth century onward the doctrine of the mystery of the Immaculate Conception spread throughout the Iberian peninsula[44] promoted by the magisterium of the church and especially by the Catholic monarchs. The Jesuit missionaries who arrived in the Americas were messengers of devotion to the Mother of God. An example of those who were caught up in this Marian missionary climate is Father José de Anchieta, S.J., beatified by Pope John Paul II on 3 July 1980; the Jesuit composed innumerable poems to the Virgin as well as a number of sermons about her.

The missionaries' catechesis always included devotion to the Virgin, and the practice of praying the rosary became a mainstay in the Catholic life of Indian villages, later in the slave quarters of blacks, and eventually it became an important tradition in Latin American popular religiosity.

What most interests us is the history of the involvement of Our Lady Aparecida with the poor, how she has accompanied them in their lives, heard their laments, and nourished their hopes. Thus "baptized" by the people because of her story, Our Lady Aparecida has entered into the life of the poor and has become their companion in the difficult road traveled every day.

From the outset popular imagination has tried to discover why the image of the Immaculate Conception was under water in the Paraíba River. Although many legends have been told to explain it, one of them is better known than the others. According to the story, the statue was thrown in the Paraíba River to chase away a huge serpent that was creating panic among the people.[45] The serpent then fled and the people could live in peace again. Before being the one who "appeared" in the waters, the image of Mary had been "thrown" in the waters to protect the people from jeopardy. Hence the story of the people's relation to Mary reaches back prior to the event of the "miraculous catch." This event gave the people's devotion a new shape and to some extent changed its direction.

The Virgin thrown into the waters was the one brought by the Portuguese colonizers: a white Virgin, even if she was sculpted on Brazilian soil. The image found in the waters is black. The waters of the Paraíba River (= *para'iva* = useless river) blacken the statue turning it the color of the abused people.[46] Poor fishermen catch it in their nets and it is reborn giving them greater power and identity, especially the blacks of that area and nearby areas who come to find in it an expression of their race, their color, their history. Rooted in this trust by the people, devotion to the new Immaculate Conception, she who was "saved from the waters," the Aparecida, has spread more and more. Now the Virgin Aparecida has become "Brazilian," as though one more identity had been added to her. That has the effect of gradually strengthening the very identity of popular religion, for to some extent the Virgin found has been born of the people.

Among the many miracles performed by the Virgin one of them is quite well known, especially by the poor. According to the story one day a slave in chains asked his master if he could pray at the door of a small shrine set up to honor the Virgin. After getting permission he began to pray at the chapel door. Right away the metal ring on his neck and the chain binding him fell off his body. Even today these things are on display at the shrine testifying to the Aparecida's love and affection for slaves.[47] This event spread by word of mouth and helped make her the protector of slaves in the Paraíba Valley, Minas Gerais,

São Paulo, and nearby regions. The Virgin who had become "black" could not but be the same one who would break unjust chains, the chains that diminished human dignity, especially for millions of people who had been uprooted from African soil and enslaved to serve the economic interests of the privileged.

Even while slavery was in force in Brazil during the eighteenth century, many interpreted this sign by the Virgin as an indicator of Mary's disapproval of slavery in our country. Once more the people were reading Mary's signs as a demand for liberation, even though this reading was not the most common one at that time.

As we know, we read signs in accordance with our desires and our economic and ideological interests. The slave owners did not perceive or grasp the Virgin's "language" in the way just mentioned. They wanted her in their chapels; they decorated her altar; and just like the slaves, they were devoted to the family rosary.

Those who wield power have always tried to take over devotion to Mary and subject the poor to their organizations and demands. Despite that, however, history attests to the fact that the people's own devotion, with the originality of its religious expression, has always managed to find a way to stay alive despite countless difficulties. Over rough roads this devotion managed to maintain a degree of independence, a tenuous expression of freedom and of the yearning for recognition and self-determination. The Black Virgin, the one who had appeared [*aparecida*] for the poor, is part of their inalienable heritage.

That is how two poets have understood and expressed it, singing of the struggle and worth of black Brazilians: the bishop-poet Pedro Casaldáliga and the composer and musician Milton Nascimento in their "Praise to Mariama" of the Missa dos Quilombos. [*Ama* is a term used among black Brazilians for wet-nurse; thus "Mariama" assimilates Mary to the figure of the black nanny. *Quilombos* were settlements formed by runaway slaves, the most famous being Palmares—trans.] Some of the words of these poets are:

> Sing on the mountaintop your prophecy
> That overthrows the rich and the powerful, O Mary,

Raise up those held down, mark the renegades,
Dance the samba in the joy of many feet.

Give strength to our shouts,
Raise our sights,
Gather the slaves in new Palmares,
Come down once more to the nets of life
of your black people, black Aparecida.

7. BY WAY OF CONCLUSION

In order to speak of the many Latin American faces of Mary, we would need hundreds of volumes. We would have to go on pilgrimage to her countless shrines, try to sense the soul of those devoted to her, especially in the "holy places" of this devotion, in order to express some further aspects of this religious treasure, the heritage of a people.

We would have to visit Luján in Argentina, Chiquinquirá in Colombia; we would have to become acquainted with La Purísima, the Immaculate Conception, who is called "La Linda" in Cuzco, Purísima in Nicaragua, the Virgin of Guápulo in Quito, Our Lady of Caridad del Cobre in Cuba, Our Lady of Altagracia in the Dominican Republic, and so many other names that it is rash to cite these names without all the others.[48]

The same song of praise intoned to her whom the people have chosen as Mother and Protector, as Mistress and Guide, can be heard in different tonalities and rhythms making up a single symphony of a pilgrim people hoping and struggling for its liberation.

CHAPTER VI

Mary and God's Wonders among the Poor

In some earlier chapters in this book we went over what scripture and church tradition say about the person of Mary and attempted to elucidate some presuppositions and elements for a Marian theology more suited to our time and situation; in Chapter V we went on to consider some aspects of the history of the deep relationship between this woman—whom the church venerates as Our Lady—and the humble people of our land who view her and love her as their dear Mother, infinitely kind, "our life, our sweetness, and our hope." Our reflection on the appearances, cures, and miracles—and more specifically on the appearance of the Virgin of Guadalupe, "Dark-skinned Mother of Heaven, Our Lady of Latin America," and of the black Aparecida, in the waters of the Paraíba River—sought to bring out the relevance of our people's immense devotion to Mary for any theological reflection today on our continent. In Latin America one cannot speak about the church of the poor or of pastoral work among the popular classes without dealing with the figure of this woman who carried the Liberator of the poor in her womb and gave birth to him.

Therefore it is even less possible to speak of the organizing and struggle for liberation taking place in Latin America without turning our eyes toward Mary and seeing what message her person and her mystery provide today in the communities and groups who are striving for and living out this organizing and this struggle. How do they see Mary, how do they pray to her, what songs do the people in the base Christian communities sing to her, this oppressed people journeying in search of the promised land and struggling for its liberation? And how can this Marian piety and devotion experienced in base communities shed light on the journey of the poor, while at the same time criticizing and purifying the stereotypes imposed by traditional Marian devotion?[1]

1. BASE CHRISTIAN COMMUNITIES AND DEVOTION TO MARY

Base communities, which are growing every day in our country and continent, are no doubt signs that hope is smiling on the Latin American church. A great deal has been written about them, whole books, doctoral theses, indeed whole libraries.[2] It is not our intention at this point to add to this extensive bibliography. Rather we intend to devote some consideration to the new ecclesiological fact that the base communities represent for the church in Latin America and to grasp the implications this may have for our understanding of, and relationship to, Mary within this people, now becoming organized in a new way of being church.

Base communities embody concretely the thrust of the church. That thrust is rooted in God's word, in history and tradition, and it is gradually revealed in many ways. As time goes on it continues to take on new forms, which are always original within their very plainness and ordinariness, as those forms take shape among the poor and suffering people who meet to ponder and celebrate their lives and their struggles in the light of God's word. That is why the base communities are good news. Mary also was and is the embodiment of a thrust of the church in the midst of the poor, the thrust toward a new humankind which God the Creator is lovingly and patiently bringing about, the thrust which as time goes on is taking the startling and radically new form of God's breaking into human history.

Base communities take shape in the midst of the poor. On the basis of what is socially insignificant and disdained by those in high positions, God is making the gospel of salvation resound and is renewing the church on this continent. Mary is—also and nothing but—a poor woman and socially insignificant.[3] Together with Jesus and Joseph she forms an upright and humble family struggling to live, their bread earned by hard work every day, a family utterly faithful to the tendency among the Israelites known as the "poor of Yahweh." It is on the basis of her poverty and unimportance—besides her moral virtues and human qualities—that God sows in her the seed of the liberation of a whole people and exalts her before all generations as "blessed."

The base communities are prophetic church, taking shape in the midst of conflicts. These small groups of people who are poor and unimportant, who take their inspiration from the gospel, disturb the powerful, and they are defamed and calumniated by some, while others envy them and want to manipulate them. In the midst of these interwoven conflicts, the base communities keep trying to cut out their own path and always regain their bearings from their fidelity to the God of life who has called them and brought them together. In a similar manner, conflict was always latent throughout Mary's whole experience, as the Gospels narrate it.[4] She went through a "different" and unique kind of gestation and gave birth in the midst of the strains created by the Roman occupation force, far from her own land and relatives, an exile and uprooted with her newborn son. She was a follower of this same son in his project of forging a Kingdom, and then her son fell out of favor with the religious and civil authorities of that period, and she became the mother of the one sentenced and crucified. Thus Mary represents the people faithful to God, bearing oppression and persecution so the Light may shine and liberation may become reality. It is in the heart of the dialectical tension between anguish and hope, between love and suffering, that Mary and the people of the base communities lift their prophetic cry to denounce injustice and announce the liberation that has already taken place, and is now taking place for those who hope in Yahweh.

In their characteristic features, base Christian communities are:

—*true communities*—united by family-type bonds, with a deep relationship between their members;

—*ecclesial*—they are set up and linked together on the basis of Christian faith and bonds of communion with the whole church;

—*base* [grassroots]—their members come from the popular classes and are poor and humble, generally from the rural areas or from the outskirts of large cities.

Hence, in them the divine and the popular are indissolubly linked. They belong to God and belong to the people; they are God's irruption into the people as they struggle and organize for their liberation.

Likewise, Mary is:

—*totally God's*—she personifies those who are disposed to hear God's word, who hear it, accept it, and put it into practice. She is the voice for this God who raises up the poor and overthrows the powerful. She is an active member in the first community that follows and is identified with Jesus' project of the Kingdom of God, and that after the resurrection comes together under the breath of the Spirit. Her hearing is entirely open to God, to God's word and inspiration.

—*totally the people's*—poor and humble by birth, Mary of Nazareth really belongs to the popular classes. Therefore, the New Testament authors see in her the personification of the chosen people itself—that faithful Israel which from the time of the Old Testament onward journeyed in pursuit of Yahweh's promises and in whose midst the new Israel finds the conditions and fertile soil for being born. Since she is fully from the people, and of the people, Mary can be the one who bears in herself the salvation for which this very people so longs and yearns. A woman of true fidelity—to God and to the people—she awaits and proclaims God's manifestation as liberation of the humiliated and the starving.[5]

It is understandable therefore that the base communities should be ever mindful of Mary in their ongoing life and struggles. In the theological reflection that flows from their concrete practice, Mary has become a symbol of the hope that nourishes the poor along their way. Some writers[6] believe that it is still premature to speak of a "following" of Mary, and we agree. "For most of the population, and even in base communities, The Mother of Heaven, holy and merciful, still seems to outweigh our sister on earth, striving to re-establish justice and build the Kingdom."[7] Nevertheless there are already real signs of this experience of Mary as a companion along the way. She who is invoked as "Mother of the Oppressed," "Our Lady of Latin America," "Mother of the Forgotten," is also traveling along with the people when they sing:

> Oh, come walking along with us,
> Holy Mary, come.
> Oh, come walking along with us,
> Holy Mary, come.

The Sixth Interchurch Gathering of Base Communities in Trindade, Goiás, Brazil, held in July 1986 calls her "companion in our journey." All the poor people meeting there, linked in the same faith and same struggle, sign off in the document that contains their conclusions "renewed in hope and in the company of Mary, the mother of Jesus and of our martyrs." Together with those who have spilled their blood for the lives of their brothers and sisters, Mary is the one who accompanies the people's journey toward the promised land.

Hence she is the one forging a new spirituality, and she is a model for it, a spirituality that springs from the "well" of the life, suffering, and joys of the people of Latin America.[8] Bible study groups observe and meditate on her example, starting from the simple and sparse Bible passages that mention her. Her strong and unwavering faith, her praxis of effective and practical love as she goes to aid her pregnant cousin, to make sure that the party is not ruined for lack of wine, to persevere in prayer with the group of timid and frightened disciples—all these are a stimulus for the members of the communities, helping to propel them forward in their struggle, to bolster them to fight their fight and sing their song in the painful and heavy everyday effort of life. If, as the Council says, Mary is a figure of the church, we can say that here in Latin America she is increasingly the figure of this church of the poor, of which the base communities are a new and outstanding embodiment.

Paul VI's document *Marialis Cultus* energetically states that Mary of Nazareth, "far from being a passively submissive woman or one with an alienating religiosity, was indeed a woman who did not hesitate to say that God is the one who vindicates the poor and the oppressed and who has cast the powerful off their thrones" (MC 37). This same perspective is taken up again by the Puebla document (293):

> She is not just the admirable fruit of the redemption; she is also the active co-worker in it. Mary shows quite clearly that Christ does not annul the creativity of those who follow him. She is Christ's partner, who develops all her human capabilities and responsibilities to the point where she becomes the new Eve alongside the new Adam. By virtue of her freely proffered cooperation in Christ's new covenant, Mary is the protagonist of history alongside him.

In Latin America where the poor are every day becoming more aware of their situation of oppression and, motivated by their deep faith, are uniting in solidarity and becoming organized in pursuit of liberation, Mary is not only their traveling companion but also the voice of their yearning and hope.

2. THE MAGNIFICAT: SONG OF MARY, SONG OF THE PEOPLE

As we conclude our essay in Marian theology we return to something we see as extremely important, Mary's song, the Magnificat (Luke 1:46–55).[9] We are aware that we have mentioned it and commented and reflected on it throughout this study. However, we want to pause once more over this New Testament text because we think it is fundamental for a better understanding of Marian piety in Latin America. This piety is a prior and indispensable datum for the Marian theology we are trying to do.

Mary, whom the Spirit makes pregnant because she has given her assent, is the same woman on whose lips is placed the prophetic and liberating canticle of the Magnificat. Mary's obedience to God's enterprise goes hand in hand with her opposition to anything opposed to this enterprise: sin, the forces of the anti-Kingdom with their diabolical wiles and their many-tentacled depravity. Thus her person—the "daughter of Sion," prototypical figure of the faithful people—is the channel both of God's "yes" to the people and of God's "no" to the forces that hinder that same people from living the covenant with their God.

The Puebla document says, "The Magnificat mirrors the soul of Mary. In that canticle we find the culmination of the spirituality of Yahweh's poor and lowly, and of the prophetic strain in the Old Testament. It is the opening proclamation of Christ's new Gospel, the prelude to the Sermon on the Mount" (297). In his homily in Zapopán, Mexico, Pope John Paul II points to Mary as a model for those "who do not passively accept the adverse circumstances of personal and social life and are not victims of alienation, as they say today, but who with her proclaim that God 'raises up the lowly' and, if necessary 'overthrows the powerful from their thrones.' "[10] In his recent encyclical *Redemptoris Mater* the Pope states:

> The church, which even "amid trials and tribulations" does not cease repeating with Mary the words of the Magnificat, is sustained by the power of God's truth, proclaimed on that occasion with such extraordinary simplicity. At the same time, by means of this truth about God the church desires to shed light upon the difficult and sometimes tangled paths of humankind's earthly existence (RM, 37, 2).

It is in pursuit of this "illumination" that we will strive to set this text in its historical and eschatological context, seeking to analyze it in literary and theological terms.

(a) Eschatological and Historical Context

The purpose of the canticles of the proto-history of Christianity—the Magnificat (Luke 1:46–55), Benedictus (Luke 1:67–79) and Nunc Dimittis (Luke 2:29–33)—which appear in Luke's Gospel is to shed light on the historic and spiritual meaning of the advent of the incarnation of the Word. As the leading figure in the Magnificat, Mary is presented as the servant of the Lord—prototypical figure of Israel consoled and set free, the one chosen for this historical and eschatological event of salvation which has come for God's people.

Hence the canticle Luke places on her lips cannot be understood as something she sings for herself as an individual, but must rather be seen as sung for the messianic people, the people yearning and sighing for the promises of the Lord God. Not simply a hymn of praise and thanksgiving, the Magnificat is nothing less than a meditation in poetic form on the wonders God works in the history of salvation. These wonders have reached their high point with the arrival of the Word on earth in human flesh (see Chapter III, above).

Written after A.D. 70, at a time when the first generation of martyrs was giving living witness with its blood, Luke's Gospel naturally interprets the pre-paschal events in the light of post-paschal events and experiences. Hence, the canticles in this Gospel do not seek to reflect merely the internal feelings of those who speak them, but they are the voice of the whole church which sees itself in them.

In these songs there is a whole range of varied and contradictory human feelings—from joyful thanksgiving to acknowledgment of the misery and injustice ruling the world, from the most loving docility and acceptance of God's saving word to the sharpest and most conscious rebellion against all forms of institutionalized sin. These feelings resound with complex polyphony in the great saving event where Mary's poverty is joined to the divine wealth. Mary—she who has believed and hence is blessed—now lends her voice to all those who have hoped in the Redeemer, the Messiah, the consolation of Israel, and who re-read the events of their history with eyes turned to the present and toward the future of God's promise which is now becoming reality.

The themes developed in the text—the salvation that comes from the house of David, fulfillment of the covenant made with Abraham, the raising up of the poor—are common in the catechesis carried out in the Jewish-Christian community. In this text, as elsewhere in his Gospel and in Acts (see 6:20–22; 23:46; Acts 5:31), the evangelist reveals his special feeling for the poor, the lowly, and the outcast—concrete and real persons who are the victims of all kinds of injustice and oppression. With the event of Jesus Christ, these people are victorious over those who cause their misery and oppression.[11]

(b) The Paradox of Mary's Song

The decisive event of the incarnation of the Word of God is both paradoxical and subversive. Occurring in the body and life of Mary of Nazareth, woman and symbol of the whole people, this event is filled with social, ethical, and religious implications, despite what is exceptional and unique about it. By dividing the text of the Magnificat into (1) a positive part (vv. 46–50, 54–5), and (2) a negative part (vv. 51–3), we can better grasp these implications.

The first part of the canticle (vv. 46–50 and taken up again in the final vv. 54–5) expresses the people's acceptance of God's infinite gift which at this moment is present as a seed in the fertile womb of Mary of Nazareth. The *fiat* that the Lord's servant gives to the messenger's announcement (Luke 1:38) opens the gates to the inrush of the Spirit who initiates the fullness of time (see Gal. 4:4) and the new creation in human history. The opening verses of the Magnificat express this faith of Mary who opens herself unconditionally to God's grace and sees herself as the vessel of God's wonders ("... God *my* savior"). This faith of Mary's, however, is none other than Israel's faith in the holy and all-powerful God, whose gratuitous mercy continues from Abraham, Sarah, Hagar, and the faith of the fathers and mothers of the people, through Moses, Miriam, and the prophets and prophetesses; this is a faith in God for whom nothing is impossible and who has placed in the Virgin's womb a son whose name will be Jesus (Jeshua = Yahweh saves), for he will liberate the people from their sins (see Matt. 1:21).

After the "yes" given in the obscurity of faith at the annunciation (Luke 1:38) there comes the "yes" that is full of joy over God's wonders now being performed in history: "Yes! From now on all generations will call me blessed, for the Almighty has done great things for me!" (Luke 1:48–9). These great things done by the holy and almighty God go in the same direction as the whole complex of favors given by Yahweh to the people all the time. The God who formed the Messiah in Mary's womb, making her the vessel of salvation, is the same God who made possible the exodus from Egypt and the reconstituting of the people after the experience of dismemberment during the exile. Mary's "yes," Israel's "yes"—both are *servants* of the Lord (see vv. 48, 54)—is an echo of human faith in the primordial and continual "yes" of God who chooses, reveals, and loves first, and who, consistent with and faithful to God's usual way of acting, looks lovingly on what is small, humiliated, and scorned in this world. God favors the humiliation of God's servant (v. 48) and bends down toward Israel, which is afflicted and needs help (v. 54).

The other half of the canticle, however, sets us squarely in the middle of the subversive and conflictive paradox of a God who, while acting in favor of God's people, takes sides and wields a strong arm against those who try to exercise any kind of oppression against this same people. While saying a loving "yes," this God also says a vigorous "no." And Mary, the mild Virgin of the "yes," she whom traditional catechesis has over and over again presented as the passive and silent mother of the Child Jesus, comes out as someone who stands up and clearly and valiantly takes on as her own this God's "no" (see Puebla, 297).

The concrete sign of the sub-version and re-versal of the established order wrought by the incarnation of the Word and the new practice of the Kingdom is the raising up of the weak, the disinherited, the "poor of Yahweh"; the reversal of the positions that the powerful have greedily taken for themselves illustrates and highlights the new social order set up through God's saving action. Those who have become rich (*ploutountes*) through tricky paths of exploitation and injustice and those who use their power to oppress and tyrannize (*dynastai*) are treated with severity by this God who spreads God's generosity and gifts among the hungry (*peinōntes*) and the humble (*tapeinoi*). Between the arrogant and the *anawim*—the poor who fear God—the divine heart inclines toward the latter and looks on their affliction.[12] In order to aid them and pull them out of their situation of misery, God must put a stop to the disordinate ambitions of the former.

The evangelist does not mince words in communicating this mercy of God toward the most abandoned of God's children.

God does not wait until the end of time before acting very concretely. Starting now God begins to register a resounding "no" to any kind of sin that impedes or blocks the Kingdom of justice and freedom from arriving. God's "no" resounds powerfully over the pride of the haughty, the ambition of the powerful, and the stuffed bellies of the rich. God scatters some, overthrows others, sends others away. In doing so, God seals this "no" to the established order in this world where those who hold power claim to have the last word.

The evangelist places this "no" of God on Mary's lips. This woman of faith, symbol of the people, who, overshadowed by the Most High, has offered both her bodiliness and her spirit so as to be permeated by the Spirit and receive the Word in her womb, stands up fearlessly and sings out with her song of freedom. Thus she reproduces in time and space the activity and song of those women who within Israel had proclaimed the strong arm of the Lord's justice.

On the way out of Egypt, the land of slavery, Miriam sings, "Sing to the Lord, for he is gloriously triumphant; horse and chariot he has cast into the sea" (Exod. 15:21). Hannah, whose sterility has been made fruitful through God's power, also gives praise: "The bows of the mighty are broken, / while the tottering gird on strength" (1 Sam. 2:4). The judge and prophetess Deborah, who urges Barak to take Sisara, for she is certain that he will have Yahweh's protection in this war-making task, sings over the victory: "May all your enemies perish thus, O Lord! / but your friends be as the sun rising in its might!" (Judg. 5:31). The beautiful Judith has dressed up and adorned herself, enhancing her womanly charms in order to seduce and defeat the enemy general Holofernes, who has been threatening the peace of her people. After cutting off his head, she declares, "Praise God, who has not withdrawn his mercy from the house of Israel, but has shattered our enemies by my hand this very night" (Jth. 13:14).

The women of Israel, among whom Mary is both a legitimate heir and also one who creates and does new things, are instruments of the "yes" of God who announces and promises that new times are coming. But they also announce and effect the "no" of this same God to the forces of the anti-Kingdom that threaten to destroy God's saving enterprise. A voice for the poor and humble, God's favorites, Mary can speak and sing because she is herself poor and humble, like Israel, God's people. Thus she interprets the yearnings of these *anawim* of God, the socio-political and religious aspirations of the outcasts and the national yearnings of the Jewish people.[13] God's "no" resounding from Mary's lips is a "no" to the social evil of injustice in its various forms and thus to the theological evil of sin.

There is a counterpart to Mary's continual "yes" to God and God's plan, another side of the coin: Mary's "no" to injustice and to the state of things with which there can be no compromise. This is Mary's "no" to the sin of alienation, to what is not done when others are being victimized and are suffering. Mary, figure of the faithful people, servant of the Lord, is also the prophetic woman bearing in herself God's words and the aspirations of the people, and in her speech and life she denounces sin and announces the covenant. Mary's solidarity with God's saving plan and with the people's aspiration for liberation are in accordance with her firm opposition to injustice that oppresses and kills.

It is therefore incumbent on the church of the poor, which is embodied today in the course taken by the base communities, to reflect ever more on the person and mystery of Mary within its context of oppression, struggle, resistance, and victory. Reflecting and working out a new kind of theological discourse — whose starting point will be the concrete and patient experience and practice of the daily life of the people vis-à-vis the mystery of Mary — will entail that this same church turn to look at itself, to look at its identity and mission. If the church earnestly compares itself with the person and figure of Mary, such reflection will entail examining and discerning whether it has truly said "yes" and whether it has had the courage to say "no" at the right time. It will entail diagnosing its witness and what it has done in prophecy and evangelizing; it will even entail examining what it has done in the face of martyrdom. It will mean evaluating itself on its commitment to announcing the good news to the poor and denouncing anything that prevents this good news from becoming reality.

God's preferential love for the poor is admirably set forth in

Mary's Magnificat. "The God of the covenant, of whom the Virgin of Nazareth sings in exultation, is also the one who 'casts down the powerful from their thrones and raises up the humble; fills the hungry with good things and sends the rich away empty-handed; . . . [and] scatters the proud. . . . His love extends forever over those who fear him,' " says John Paul II (RM 37, 3). He continues:

> Drawing from Mary's heart, from the depth of her faith expressed in the words of the Magnificat, the church renews ever more effectively in herself the awareness that the truth about God who saves, the truth about God who is the source of every gift, cannot be separated from the manifestation of his love of and preference for the poor and humble, that love which, celebrated in the Magnificat, is later expressed in the words and works of Jesus.
>
> The church is thus aware — and at the present time this awareness is particularly vivid — not only that these two elements of the message contained in the Magnificat cannot be separated, but also that there is a duty to safeguard carefully the importance of "the poor" and of "the option in favor of the poor" in the word of the living God. These are matters and questions intimately connected with the Christian meaning of freedom and liberation (RM 37, 3–4).

The Congregation for the Doctrine of the Faith's *Instruction on Christian Freedom and Liberation* (March 22, 1986) states: "It is to Mary as mother and model that the church must look in order to understand in its completeness the meaning of her own mission" (97).[14]

It is through Mary that the church will always have to strive to be converted every day so as to be ever more the servant of the Lord in whom wondrous things are done.

CHAPTER VII

Conclusion

Having come to the end of our essay in Marian theology based on women and Latin America, we will now attempt to look back on the road we have taken in order to single out some concluding points. In doing this we are nevertheless aware that in matters of theology and the mystery that is the object of its reflection it is almost impossible to get to the end of a road or to define concepts. We certainly intend, however, to blaze a trail so that other men and women may be able to continue to think and move ahead following what we – humbly – have attempted to say.

As regards our methodology, we first tried to situate the perspective from which we were speaking. Thus in *Chapter I* we tried to describe the anthropological assumptions guiding us. We wanted to overcome the most common anthropological shortcomings – male-centrism, dualism, idealism, one-dimensionalism – and so we tried to base our work on a human-centered, unifying, realist, and pluri-dimensional anthropology. Moreover, and this is most important, for our theology we consciously assumed a theological viewpoint specific to women. Since we are women, seeking to think about and organize discourse on the woman Mary, we could not but work from such a perspective.

Chapter II sought to continue situating the reader in the direction that must be taken in order to perceive what the scripture tells us of Mary. The aim of the hermeneutical clarifications in that chapter was to lay out the necessary guidemarks for reading what is in the Bible and to provide elements for a Marian theology which would be further elaborated later on. The central idea of Mary as one who "lives in God," the feminine element, and the personal factors conditioning the authors were some of these elements.

Chapter III sought to enter fully into the scriptures. The starting point was a central category: the Kingdom of God. That provided the basis for reviewing the Old and New Testaments, indicating the women in the course of the history of Israel who were outstanding bearers of God's salvation for the people. Mary is both their heir and one who begins something new. Then Mary, a woman in ancient Judaism, was set in the social, political, and economic context of her age. Finally there was a review of the very few but deep New Testament texts that explicitly mention the mother of Jesus.

Next, *Chapter IV* was an attempt at the delicate task of dealing with the tradition of the church, while keeping in mind what the scriptures say. Here we tried to re-think the Marian dogmas — an area that is ecumenically controversial and morally challenging — grounded in the spirit of our own age and within the perspective that is prevailing more and more in Latin America, from which we speak: the perspective of the poor.

Chapters V and *VI* then plunged us into the heart of our Latin America, which is replete with devotion to Mary and love for her. In Chapter V we first surveyed the history of Marian devotion on our continent; next we reflected on the phenomena of Mary's appearances, cures, and miracles, which often take place in the world of popular Catholicism; then we devoted considerable attention to Mary's appearance at Guadalupe to the Indian Juan Diego. In Chapter VI we tried to perceive what is *new* about what is happening in the midst of the poor of our continent who are organizing and struggling for their liberation, and we tried to discern how those developments affect the poor's relationship with Mary. After trying to elucidate Mary's role in the base communities' new way of being church, we reflected specifically on the Magnificat, the song of liberation of the poor of all ages, which the evangelist Luke placed on the lips of Mary of Nazareth, fearless and faithful Daughter of Sion.

As we get to the end of this whole journey, certain points stand out. These points follow from the perspective we took at the beginning, from the method we used, and from the thinking that thereby resulted:

1. In its effort to approach the mystery of Mary, traditional Mariology may run the risk of disconnecting her from the earth and from the people to whom she belongs. If and when that happens, such a Mariology fails to take into account many of the facets that the mystery of this symbol-woman, this people-woman, encompasses and reveals. The collective scope of Mary's person is lost, and what is left is an exaggerated and impoverished individualism; the aspect of kindness and acceptance that the popular intuition perceives so well can be circumscribed in a hardened and alienating rigidity.

2. A new Marian theology, on the other hand, tells us that the mystery of Mary brings a new word about the world, about this world where men and women are born, grow, love, suffer, live, clash, rejoice, and die. It says that this world is the dwelling place not only of those who "live in history" but also of those who "live in God," of those who in their situation as resurrected continue to participate and act in the lives of their brothers and sisters who sigh and struggle for liberation. Hence, the people recognize in Mary not only one who "lives in God," but also one who is in solidarity with their sorrows and joys, and they confidently invoke her: ". . . Our advocate, turn your eyes of mercy toward us. . . . " The mystery of Mary says that the world is not just a sinister stage for an absurd tragedy where victors and vanquished are ever the same, but a place where those who fight the good fight of life can hope for victory, under the merciful eyes of the Mother of Life. Their victory is guaranteed in her who is victorious in God, but who does not abandon those who acknowledge her and call on her as advocate and mother.

3. The mystery of Mary also brings a new message about the human being, a message that says that this being—made in God's image and likeness—cannot be reduced to the limits of individualism, to the narrowness of sexism, to the alienation of idealism. Mary, collective figure, symbol of the faithful people from whose womb emerges the New Creation, unfolds before human beings all their infinite horizons with their indescribable possibilities. Mary helps us rethink theological anthropology with our focus turned toward the infinite that is God. Moreover,

Mary helps the women who are her sisters and companions to rediscover their identity in the Kingdom where there is "neither Jew nor Greek, neither slave nor free, neither man nor woman." New Eve, mother of the living, thus is she invoked on the lips of those who seek in her the successful outcome of God's dream: "Hail, our life, our sweetness and our hope!"

4. Finally, the mystery of Mary brings a new word about God. Mary is the human permeated with the divine in her every recess and every aspect. Her humanity, which is entirely open and permeated, and her full participation in the enterprise of the Kingdom help us perceive who the God of this Kingdom is: God the Creator, who does not cease to perform wonders on behalf of the poor, overthrowing the powerful and filling the hungry; God the Word who resounds with invincible force, filling and making fruitful every receptive virgin womb; God the Spirit, free and liberating, blowing where it will and continually bringing about the slow, painful, and beautiful work of giving birth to a New Creation, where justice is law and the poor are privileged. In the light of this God there shines a new hope for all the oppressed of Latin America, downtrodden by dire poverty and oppression. And this hope bears the face of Mary: the servant on whom the Most High has looked with favor. Hence the people make her song their own, and with their lungs and lips express their love for Mary and her presence with them:

MARY, MARY

Mary, Mary is a gift,
a certain magic,
a power to alert us,
a woman who deserves
to live and to love
like any other on this earth.

Mary, Mary is the music,
the heart and the sweat
of a people who laugh
when they ought to be crying,
not living but merely surviving.

But we need strength
and we need pride,
strength of mind—we whose
bodies are signed
"Mary, Mary,"
a mixture of sorrow and joy.

But we need guile
and we need pride
and a dream that won't fade—
with her mark on our skin,
we're a strange, manic race:
we have faith in life.

Glossary

ARCHETYPE: basic models or ideas set back in the beginning of time, which primitive peoples utilize in order to explain and give meaning to the present. The term is used here in the context of the history of religions.

COSMOS: Greek word meaning "world."

DOXOLOGY: derives from *doxa,* Greek word meaning "glory." These are generally words of praise to God in the form of hymns, appearing in liturgical texts in the Bible and in the church's liturgy.

HYPOSTASIS: Greek word meaning subsistence, person. The church says of Jesus Christ that he is one subsistence (one person) in two natures.

KAIROS: privileged time of grace, the opposite of *chronos,* profane time.

ONTOLOGICAL: comes from "ontology," which is the study of the problem of comprehending Being and each being as the condition for the possibility of thinking and acting in relation to concrete reality: ontology studies the very being of beings.

PARTHENOGENESIS: development of a non-fecundated ovum, which results in an individual like others. Spontaneous pregnancy.

PNEUMATOLOGY: area of systematic theology that studies the third divine person, the Holy Spirit.

PROTO-EVANGELIUM: the gospel before the Gospels as such. *Proto-* means "first."

PROTO-HISTORY: history before history.

PROTOTYPE: first type or examplar; original, model.

SOTERIOLOGY: area of systematic theology that studies what is related to salvation and redemption.

TAPEINŌSIS: term that designates the poor, those who were socially unimportant in Israel. Mary applies it to herself in the Magnificat.

THEOPHANY: appearance by God.

TORAH: Hebrew word meaning "law."

ULTRAMONTANISM: doctrine and politics of French Catholics (and others) who sought inspiration and support beyond the mountains (the Alps), that is, in the Roman curia. System of those who defend the absolute authority of the Pope in the area of faith and discipline.

UTOPIA: Greek term meaning "non-place." It refers to projects in history that do not yet exist in history and hence motivate and move social forces to bring them about.

Notes

I. TOWARD A NEW ANTHROPOLOGICAL PERSPECTIVE

1. The authors use the terms "anthropology" and "anthropological" in the philosophical or theological sense of the study of what it means to be human—Trans.

2. K. E. Borresen, "L'anthropologie théologique d'Augustin et de Thomas d'Aquin," in *Recherches de Science Religieuse* 69/3 (1981).

3. See C. Boff, *Theology and Praxis: Epistemological Foundations* (Maryknoll, N.Y.: Orbis Books, 1987).

4. See J. Comblin, *O tempo da ação* (Petrópolis: Vozes, 1982).

5. P. Ricoeur, *Fallible Man* (New York: Fordham University Press, 1986).

6. Today the notion of *complementarity* is questioned by one kind of feminist theology which prefers to speak about *relationality*. See R. R. Ruether, *Sexism and God-Talk* (Boston: Beacon Press, 1983).

7. See L. Boff, *The Maternal Face of God* (San Francisco: Harper & Row, 1988).

8. *"Chamei de mau gosto o que vi, de mau gosto, mau gosto, / É que Narciso acha feio o que não é espelho...."* [What I saw seemed in bad taste, bad taste, bad taste, / For Narcissus finds ugly anything but a mirror....]

9. See E. and J. Moltmann, *Dieu, homme et femme* (Paris: Du Cerf, 1984).

10. See M. Riley, *Eve and Mary Are Stem—All Our Centuries Go Back to Them* (Washington, D.C.: Center of Concern, 1984).

11. I. Gebara, "A mulher faz teologia," *REB* (January 1986).

12. See E. Badinter, *L'un est l'autre: Des relations entre hommes et femmes* (Paris: Ed. Odile Jacob, 1986).

13. See C. Mesters, *Por trás das palavras—I* (Petrópolis: Vozes, 1974).

14. See L. Boff, *Liberating Grace* (Maryknoll, N.Y.: Orbis Books, 1979).

15. See B. Pascal, *Oeuvres Complètes,* Bibliothèque de la Pléiade (Paris: Gallimard, 1954).

16. See P. Ricoeur, "Nommer Dieu," *EtThR* 52 (1976), pp. 489–508.

II. HERMENEUTICS FOR A MARIAN THEOLOGY

1. See J. B. Libânio and M. C. Bingemer, *Escatologia Cristã* (Petrópolis: Vozes, 1985).

2. See E. Valle, et al., *Evangelização e comportamento religioso popular* (Petrópolis: Vozes, 1978).

3. See L. Boff, "Constantes antropologicas e revelação," *REB* 125 (March 1972), pp. 26–41.

4. R. Alves, *What Is Religion?* (Maryknoll, N.Y.: Orbis Books, 1984).

5. G. Gutiérrez, *We Drink From Our Own Wells* (Maryknoll, N.Y.: Orbis Books, 1984).

6. E. Schüssler Fiorenza, *In Memory of Her: A Feminist Theological Reconstruction of Christian Origins* (New York: Crossroad, 1983).

7. See P. Ricoeur, *The Conflict of Interpretations* (Evanston, Ill.: Northwestern University Press, 1974).

III. MARY IN SCRIPTURE

1. E. Schüssler Fiorenza, *In Memory of Her: A Feminist Theological Reconstruction of Christian Origins* (Evanston, Ill.: Northwestern University Press, 1974), p. 31.

2. Further on we will return to the subject matter of the Magnificat in the light of the new aspects heralded by the poor today.

3. P. Saint Yves, *As virgens mães e os nascimentos miraculosos* (Rio de Janeiro: Ed. Livraria Império, n.d.).

4. See G. Kittel, ed., *Theological Dictionary of the New Testament* (Grand Rapids, Mich.: Eerdmans, 1964), vol. 1, p. 781.

5. Ibid., pp. 781–820.

6. J. Neusner, *Le Judaïsme à l'aube du Christianisme* (Paris: Du Cerf, 1985), pp. 92–93. Eng.: *Judaism in the Beginning of Christianity* (Philadelphia: Fortress, 1984).

7. J. Jeremias, *Jerusalem in the Time of Jesus* (Philadelphia: Fortress, 1969), pp. 363–64.

8. Ibid., p. 364, transcribing a laconic Jewish phrase: "Certain men marry off their daughters and put themselves to some expense; others marry them off and receive money for them."

9. See ibid., pp. 367–68.

10. See ibid., p. 369.

11. Kittel, *Theological Dictionary,* p. 781.

12. Jeremias, *Jerusalem,* pp. 360–61.

13. Kittel, *Theological Dictionary,* p. 777. This prayer clearly emerges in the life of official Judaism sometime around the second century.

14. Neusner, *Le Judaïsme,* p. 43.

15. J. Jeremias, *Jerusalem,* pp. 373–74.

16. S. Ben-Chorin, "A Jewish View of the Mother of Jesus", in *Concilium* 168 (Edinburgh: T & T Clark, 1983).

17. Jeremias, *Jerusalem,* p. 376.

18. The fact that subsequently the church has never been faithful to this spirit is another problem which is not under discussion here. Our object in this chapter is to consider women during this intertestamental period during which Mary lived.

19. Some place the letter to the Galatians around the year A.D. 49. Others set it around 53–4 or 56–7. In any case, the epistle to the Galatians is among the oldest documents in the whole New Testament. For more details see S. de Fiores and S. Meo, eds., *Nuovo dizionario di Mariologia* (Milan: Ed. Paoline, 1985). Article: "Bibbia."

20. On this question and on the meaning of the Greek term *adelphos* (brother), see R. E. Brown, et al., *Mary in the New Testament* (Philadelphia: Fortress, 1978), pp. 65–72. The biblical reflection in this section follows closely the exegetical studies in works such as this and the *Nuovo dizionario*, with elements from the context in which we live added to the interpretation.

21. See *Nuovo dizionario.*

22. See Schüssler Fiorenza, *In Memory of Her,* chapter 4.

23. See C. Mesters, *Palavra de Deus na história dos homens* (Petrópolis: Vozes, 1970), vol. 2.

24. E. Tamez, "Agar, a mulher que complicou a história da salvação," *Por trás da palavra,* newsletter of CEBI, no. 27 (March–April, 1985).

25. See Schüssler Fiorenza, *In Memory of Her.*

26. See Exod. 19:16. See also J. Dupont, *The Salvation of the Gentiles: Essays on the Acts of the Apostles* (New York: Paulist, 1979): "The unanimity of the Christian community at Pentecost corresponds to the assembly of Israel at the foot of Sinai."

27. Schüssler Fiorenza, *In Memory of Her.*

28. Acts 1 and 2.

29. See *Nuovo dizionario,* art.: "Bibbia."

30. Scripture speaks of another Cana, Kanah of the tribe of Asher (Josh. 19:28).

31. See *Nuovo dizionario.*

32. The fourth Gospel puts this prophecy in the mouth of Caiphas, the high priest during the time when Jesus was condemned to death.

33. The explanation for this is given in R. Brown, et al., *Mary in the New Testament.*

34. See Gen. 1:14–19; Col. 2:16.

35. Wisd. of Sol. 3:7; Dan. 12:3; Matt. 13:43.

36. See Brown, et al., *Mary in the New Testament,* chap. 8.

37. Ibid.

38. On this point see ibid., p. 239, n. 521: "Yet the picture remains nuanced here as well, for Revelation was a relatively late comer into the canon of some sections of the Eastern churches, so that this 'canonical' Marian symbolism would not be equally ancient in all areas."

IV. MARIAN DOGMAS: THEIR NEW MEANING ARISING FROM THE POOR AND THE "SPIRIT" OF OUR AGE

1. Mariology is one of the central points of contention between Catholics, Protestants, and Orthodox. See S. de Fiores and S. Meo, eds., *Nuovo dizionario di Mariologia* (Milan: Ed. Paoline, 1985). Article: "Dogmi."

2. See the recent polemic over Jean-Luc Godard's film *Hail Mary* and its controversial references to the dogmas of Mary's virginity and immaculate conception.

3. See L. Boff, *O rosto materno de Deus* (Petrópolis: Vozes, 1979), p. 15. Eng. trans.: *The Maternal Face of God* (San Francisco: Harper and Row, 1988).

4. See what Boff says in *O rosto,* p. 18: "We are probably not far from the day when women will develop systematic Mariology in light of the feminine as realized both in themselves and, in its perfection, in the Mother of God and our Mother. Surely that image of Mary will be shaped very differently from the one I will sketch." The section on dogma which follows is based, sometimes with literal quotes, on *Nuovo dizionario,* followed by a re-reading based on the presuppositions set out above. Dealing with official church teaching as we are here, it seemed wise to follow a good accepted version of the dogmatic formulations. It might seem strange that, after criticizing traditional Mariology for being based virtually exclusively on texts written by men, we should use them so widely here. This is partly because there are no Mariological works written by women or from a different viewpoint, but mainly because the texts used here come not from men or women but from scripture and the tradition of the church, and therefore belong

to the whole church and the whole of humanity. We therefore feel quite justified in using this work extensively in this section, re-reading it later with our own eyes.

5. Boff, *O rosto,* p. 138.

6. Although references to Mary's virginity appear in official documents from antiquity onward, the explicit proclamation of "before, during and after birth" was made by Paul IV in 1555, as we will note below.

7. See Chapter III.

8. This is a literal Latin translation of the original Greek. Subsequent Latin texts have a different translation: *"Et incarnatus est de Spiritu Sancto et ex Maria Virgine."* On this point see *Nuovo dizionario,* pp. 813–14.

9. Latin translation of *Theotokos.*

10. On this theme see A. Roy's beautiful reflection, "O mistério da mulher," *Convergência* 13, no. 135 (September 1980), pp. 415–21.

11. See Boff, *O rosto,* p. 15; and *Nuovo dizionario,* pp. 1438–39.

12. See Midrash on Ps. 7, no. 18, in William Braude, trans., *The Midrash on Psalms* (New Haven: Yale University Press, 1959), vol. 1, p. 117.

13. On this point see *Nuovo dizionario,* pp. 1428–31.

14. Matt. 1:21–31; Luke 1:35, 39–43, 44–56; John 1:1, 13:1

15. R. Laurentin, *Les évangiles de l'enfance du Christ* (Paris: DDB, 1982), pp. 475–76.

16. On this process in the early centuries of the church, see *Nuovo dizionario,* pp. 1454–62.

17. On this point, see A. Sicari, *Matrimonio e verginità nella Rivelazione: L'uomo frente a la gelosia di Dio* (Milan: Jaca Book, n.d.), pp. 120–21.

18. See Boff, *O rosto,* p. 163.

19. The expression is that of A. Roy, from the article cited above, p. 420.

20. See F. X. Durrwell, *El Espíritu Santo en la Iglesia* (Salamanca, Sígueme, 1986) p. 192.

21. St. Augustine, "De natura et gratia," 42, PL 44, 267. On this development of the understanding of faith with regard to Mary's freedom from sin, see *Nuovo dizionario*, p. 682.

22. Boff, *O rosto,* p. 141.

23. *Nuovo dizionario,* p. 703.

24. See the Canticle of the Magnificat, which speaks of the *tapeinōsis* (poverty) of Mary, the handmaid of the Lord.

25. Tondini (Rome, 1954, pp. 617–19) cited in *Nuovo dizionario,* article: "Assunta."

26. Ibid.

27. We have already commented on this text and its theological implications in Chapter III.

28. On this topic see *Nuovo dizionario,* article: "Apocrifi."

29. For a detailed review of the history of the dogma, see *Nuovo dizionario,* article: "Assunta."

30. *Nuovo dizionario,* p. 170.

31. Boff, *O rosto,* p. 180.

32. V. Codina, "Mariología desde los pobres," in *De la modernidad a la solidaridad* (Lima: CEP, 1985), p. 195: "Despite John XXIII's desire for the development of an ecclesiology of the church of the poor, it cannot honestly be said that Vatican II made the poor the face of the conciliar church. It is only logical that its Mariology could not be of the people and sensitive to the problems of the poor. Vatican II draws on the best of the European theology of that period, such as the Rahnerian theology on Mary as 'the one perfectly redeemed' or that of O. Semmelroth on Mary as type of the church, but it proves incapable of bringing Mariology once more close to the poor and to the people's faith."

33. Ibid., p. 205.

34. Ibid., p. 206.

35. P. Ricoeur, *The Symbolism of Evil* (Boston: Beacon Press, 1969).

V. SOME TRADITIONS OF DEVOTION TO MARY IN LATIN AMERICA

1. See R. V. Ugarte, *Historia del culto a María en Iberoamérica,* vol. 1, 3rd ed. (Madrid, 1956), p. 27.

2. Ibid., p. 11.

3. Ibid., p. 15.

4. Ibid., p. 15.

5. *História geral da Igreja na América Latina,* vol 2: E. Hoornaert, *História da Igreja no Brasil, 1ª epoca* (Petrópolis: Vozes, 1977). See also Hoornaert, *Formação do Catolicismo Brasileiro* (Petrópolis: Vozes, 1978).

6. See J. Lafaye, *Quetzalcóatl y Guadalupe: La formación de la conciencia nacional de México* (Madrid: Fondo de Cultura Economica, 1977).

7. Ibid., p. 299.

8. Ibid., p. 300.

9. See Hoornaert, *História.*

10. Ugarte, *Historia,* p. 106.

11. For example it is said that the battle of Guararapes in 1649 (Recife, Brazil) against the Dutch presence in Brazil was won under the protection and favor of Nossa Senhora dos Prazeres.

12. See S. Buarque de Holanda, and P. M. Campos, *História geral da civilização Brasileira II — O Brasil monárquico,* vol. 4: *Declínio e queda do império* (São Paulo: Difusão Européia do Livro, 1971), pp. 317–67.

13. See S. Buarque de Holanda, *Raízes do Brasil* (Rio de Janeiro: Livraria José Olympio Editora, 1973).

14. See Chapter VI of this book.

15. See "Novena a la Purísima María de Nicaragua" (Managua: Centro Ecuménico Antonio Valdivieso, 1982).

16. See "María, esperanza nuestra" (Managua: Centro Ecuménico Antonio Valdivieso, 1982).

17. See R. Laurentin, *Miracles in El Paso?* (Ann Arbor, Mich.: Servant Books, 1982).

18. See J. Brustoloni, *A Senhora da Conceição Aparecida,* 4th ed. (Aparecida: Ed. Santuário, 1984).

19. See P. Ricoeur, *The Symbolism of Evil* (Boston: Beacon Press, 1969).

20. For example, we recall Teresa of Avila, John of the Cross, Ignatius Loyola, among others.

21. See Pius XI, *Pascendi.* See also E. Schillebeeckx, *Mary: Mother of the Redemption,* 2nd ed. (London and New York: Sheed and Ward, 1984).

22. See R. L. Benedetti, "A devoção a Nossa Senhora e as transformações sociais," *Vida Pastoral* (May–June 1985). See also *SEDOC* 15/160.

23. See Chapter IV, n. 6, of this book.

24. See R. Alves, *What Is Religion?* (Maryknoll, N.Y.: Orbis Books, 1984).

25. See Exod. 3:1f.

26. See Santa Teresa de Jesus, *Libro de la vida,* in *Obras completas* (Madrid: BAC, 1979). Eng.: *The Complete Works of St. Teresa of Jesus* (London: Sheed and Ward, 1982).

27. See the well-known poem by the recently beatified Jesuit José de Anchieta; the poem was originally written on the sand of Iperoig beach (Ubatuba, coast of São Paulo region).

28. See Rev. 12:1. See our commentary, Chapter III.

29. Ugarte, *Historia,* p. 65.

30. Ibid., vol. 2.

31. Lafaye, *Quetzalcóatl,* p. 317. We note the discussion about the Virgin of Copacabana in Peru. According to some authors devotion to

the Virgin of Copacabana was subsequent to the sculpting of her statue by the Indian, Tito Yupanqui. See also P. Canova, *Guadalupe dalla parte degli ultimi* (Vicenza: Ed. Istituto San Gaetano, 1984).

32. Clodomiro Siller, *El metodo de la evangelización en el Nican Mopohua,* in the *Iglesia y Religión* series (México: Centro Antonio de Montesinos, n.d.). See also V. Elizondo, *La Morenita: Evangelizadora de las Américas* (Liguori, Mo.: Liguori Publications, 1981).

33. Ugarte, *Historia,* pp. 163–77. See also A. Junco, *Un radical problema Guadalupano* (México: Ed. Jus, 1971).

34. See Exod. 3:1a; Isa. 6:1; and elsewhere.

35. See Lafaye, *Quetzalcóatl,* p. 299.

36. Ibid., p. 329. Tonantzin, which means cobra woman, is often called Cihuacóatl. She is considered the mother of the gods and of the Mexicans.

37. In her book *In Memory of Her* (New York: Crossroad, 1983), Schüssler Fiorenza does such a reconstruction starting from the biblical tradition.

38. Ugarte, *Historia,* p. 169.

39. See Jer. 23:10; 17:5; Isa. 14:28–32; etc.

40. See M. Eliade, *The Sacred and the Profane: The Nature of Religion* (New York: Harper & Row, 1961).

41. Quetzalcóatl, regarded as the good spirit of the Indians, who opposed human sacrifice, predicted the conquest as a great cataclysm that would befall the Mexican people. He was persecuted for his belief in a single Creator God, died, rose to the heavens, and promised to return to restore his kingdom. Quetzalcóatl was believed to have been born of a virgin. His life has significant similarities to that of Jesus, so much so that many missionaries believed that the apostle Thomas had previously evangelized Mexico. Similarities to Christianity found in the religion of the Indians were regarded as the product of a pre-evangelization which had deteriorated a good deal at the time of the conquest. In some traditions Quetzalcóatl came to be identified with Saint Thomas (see Lafaye, *Quetzalcóatl,* pp. 226–27). There is a similar tradition in Brazil and in other Latin American countries such as Peru and Paraguay. It was believed that the apostle Saint Thomas had evangelized not only the East Indies, but also some parts of South America and the West Indies. There was talk of the apostle's footsteps, of crosses, and of miraculous springs, especially in Bahia. These were expressions of Indian culture which, due to their similarity to Christian symbols, were interpreted as signs of an initial evangelization of the future countries of the Americas. On this question, see S. Buarque de Holanda, *Visão do paraiso* (São Paulo: CEN, 1969).

42. See Hoornaert, *História*, p. 401.

43. See Brustoloni, *A Senhora*, p. 16.

44. See J. E. Martins Terra, *Nuestra Señora de América: El santuario de la Aparecida*, Colección Mariológica del V Centenario, no. 16 (Bogotá: CELAM, 1986).

45. See Brustoloni, *A Senhora*, p. 33.

46. A. Buarque de Holanda, *Dicionário da língua Portuguesa* (Rio de Janeiro: Nova Fronteira, 1984).

47. See Brustoloni, *A Senhora*, p. 49.

48. See the work of Rubén Ugarte, already cited several times, which pulls together the history of various Latin American devotions to Mary. CELAM, as part of the preparations of the fifth centenary of the "discovery" of the Americas, has been publishing a series called "Our Lady of the Americas" [*Neustra Señora de América*]. Some short books of this series have dealt with the different Marian devotions in our countries.

VI. MARY AND GOD'S WONDERS AMONG THE POOR

1. It is not our intention here to set the base communities *alongside* or *at the head* of the common people as a whole. It is simply our impression that as the common people become organized and established in base communities—which are a new way of being church—they begin to experience an original process in which they become aware of their place in the world and of their potential for struggle. Therefore their experience brings new elements which are a potent source for theological reflection. With regard to Mary, we also believe it is worthwhile to consider specifically what the experience of base communities says about her person and her mystery so we may grasp the newness of what this may bring to our theological reflection.

2. See, A. Barreiro, *Basic Ecclesial Communities: The Evangelization of the Poor* (Maryknoll, N.Y.: Orbis Books, 1982); L. Boff, *Ecclesiogenesis* (Maryknoll, N.Y.: Orbis Books, 1986); L. Boff, *Church: Charism and Power* (New York: Crossroad, 1985); L. Boff, *E a Igreja se fez povo* (Petrópolis: Vozes, 1986); F. L. Couto Texeira, *A fé na vida: Um estudo teológico-pastoral sobre a experiência das CEBs no Brasil* (doctoral thesis defended in December 1985 at the Gregorian University in Rome).

3. To her are applied the terms *doulē* (Luke 1:38, 48) and *tapeinōsis* (Luke 1:48), which denote poverty, anonymity, and unimportance on the social scale as well as the condition of slave or humblest servant.

4. See E. León, *María y la Iglesia profética* (Lima: CEP, 1978), p. 38.

5. L. Boff, "Maria, mulher profética e liberadora: A piedade Mariana na teologia da libertação," *REB* 38, fasc. 149 (March 1978), p. 62.

6. See T. Cavalcanti, "Culto a María—tradição e renovação," *Grande Sinal* 40, no.4 (May 1986), pp. 267–78; J. B. Libânio, "Maria santíssima na perspectiva teologica atual" (Rio de Janeiro: Centro João XXIII, 1980), mimeo.

7. Cavalcanti, "Culto," p. 276.

8. G. Gutiérrez, *We Drink from Our Own Wells* (Maryknoll, N.Y.: Orbis Books, 1984).

9. Several parts of this commentary on the Magnificat have been published in *Grande Sinal,* no. 4 (May 1986), pp. 245–56.

10. John Paul II, Homily at Zapopán, 4, *AAS,* LXXI, 230.

11. See L. Boff, "Maria, mulher profética," pp. 59–61.

12. L. Boff, *O rosto materno de Deus* (Petropólis: Vozes, 1979), p. 205, n. 6. Eng. trans.: *The Maternal Face of God* (San Francisco: Harper and Row, 1988).

13. See S. de Fiores and S. Meo, eds., *Nuovo dizionario di Mariologia* (Milan: Ed. Paoline, 1985), article: "Magnificat."

14. For the English version of the instruction, see *Origins,* 15, no. 44 (April 17, 1986).

Bibliography

BOOKS

Alfaro, J. *Maria, a bem-aventurada porque acreditou.* São Paulo: Loyola, 1986.

Alves, R. *What Is Religion?* Maryknoll, N.Y.: Orbis Books, 1984.

Badinter, E. *Mother Love: Myth and Reality—Motherhood in Modern History.* New York: Macmillan, 1981.

————. *L'un est l'autre: Des relations entre hommes et femmes.* Paris: Ed. Odile Jacob, 1986.

Boff, C. *Theology and Praxis: Epistemological Foundations.* Maryknoll, N.Y.: Orbis Books, 1987.

Boff, L. *A Ave-Maria, O feminino e o Espírito Santo.* Petrópolis: Vozes, 1980.

————. *Liberating Grace.* Maryknoll, N.Y.: Orbis Books, 1979.

————. *The Maternal Face of God.* San Francisco: Harper and Row, 1988.

Bojorge, H. A. *A figura de Maria através dos Evangelistas.* São Paulo: Loyola, 1982.

Brown, R. E., et al. *Mary in the New Testament.* Philadelphia: Fortress, 1978.

Brustoloni, J. *A Senhora da Conceição Aparecida.* 4th ed. Aparecida: Ed. Santuário, 1984.

Buarque de Holanda, S. *Raízes do Brasil.* Rio de Janerio: José Olympio, 1973.

————. *Visão do paraiso.* São Paulo: CEN, 1969.

Buytendijk, F. J. J. *La femme, ses modes d'être, de paraître, d'exister.* Paris: DDB, 1967.

Chalier, C. *Les matriarches: Sarah, Rebecca, Rachel et Léa.* Paris: Du Cerf, 1985.

Codina, V. *De la modernidad a la solidaridad.* Lima: CEP, 1985.

Comblin, J. *O tempo da ação.* Petrópolis: Vozes, 1982.

De Fiores, S., and S. Meo, eds. *Nuovo dizionario di Mariologia.* Rome: Ed. Paoline, 1985.

Dupont, J. *The Salvation of the Gentiles: Essays on the Acts of the Apostles.* New York: Paulist, 1979.

Durrwell, F. X. *El Espíritu Santo en la Iglesia.* Salamanca: Sígueme, 1986.

Dussel, E. *El dualismo en la antropología de la Cristiandad.* Argentina: Ed. Guadalupe, 1974.

Eliade, M. *The Sacred and the Profane: The Nature of Religion.* New York: Harper & Row, 1961.

Elizondo, V. *La Morenita: Evangelizadora de las Américas.* Liguori, Mo.: Liguori Publications, 1981.

Evdokimov, P. *La femme et la salut du monde.* Paris: DDB, 1978.

Falgas, J. *María, la mujer.* Madrid: Co. Cul., 1966.

Freyre. G. *The Masters and the Slaves: A Study in the Development of Brazilian Civilization.* New York: Knopf, 1946.

Gama, L. V. G. *Devoção e nostalgia: Informação histórico-litúrgica sobre o Catolicismo e o culto da Virgem Maria em Minas Gerais.* Belo Horizonte: Biblioteca Publica Estadual Luiz de Bessa, 1984.

Gutiérrez, G. *We Drink From Our Own Wells: The Spiritual Journey of a People.* Maryknoll, N.Y.: Orbis Books, 1984.

História geral da Igreja na América Latina. Petrópolis: Vozes, 1977.

Hoonaert, E. *História da Igreja no Brasil, 1ª Epoca.* Petrópolis: Vozes, 1977.

————. *Formação do Catolicismo Brasileiro.* Petrópolis: Vozes, 1978.

Husserl, E. *Ideas Pertaining to a Pure Phenomenology and to a Phenomenological Philosophy.* The Hague: M. Nijhoff, 1982.

Jeremias, J. *Jerusalem in the Time of Jesus.* Philadelphia: Fortress, 1969.

John Paul II. *Redemptoris Mater.* For the English text see *Origins* 16, no. 43 (April 9, 1987).

Junco, A. *Un radical problema Guadalupano.* México, Ed. Jus, 1971.

Kittel, G., ed. *Theological Dictionary of the New Testament.* Grand Rapids: Eerdmans, 1964.

Lafaye, J. *Quetzalcóatl y Guadalupe: La formación de la conciencia nacional de México.* Madrid: Fondo de Cultura Economica, 1977.

Laurentin, R. *Les évangiles de l'enfance du Christ.* Paris: DDB, 1982.

————. *Miracles in El Paso?* Ann Arbor, Mich.: Servant Books, 1982.

————. *Court traité de théologie Mariale.* Paris: P. Lethielleux, 1959.

León, E. *María y la Iglesia profética.* Lima: CEP, 1978.

Libânio, J. B., and M. C. Bingemer. *Escatologia Cristã.* Petrópolis: Vozes, 1985.

Long, R., and R. Pierro. *L'Altra metà della Chiesa.* Rome: CNT, 1980.

Manteau-Bonamy, H. M. *Maternité divine et incarnation.* Paris: Libraire Philosophique J. Vrin, 1949.

Marins, J., et al. *Maria-liberación y comunidad eclesial de base.* México: Centro de Reflexion Teologica, 1986.

Mesters, C. *Maria, a Mãe de Jesus.* Petrópolis: Vozes, 1979.

———. *Palavra de Deus na história dos homens.* Petrópolis: Vozes, 1984.

———. *Por trás das palavras.* Petrópolis: Vozes, 1974.

Moloney, F. *Woman, First among the Faithful.* London: Darton, Longman, and Todd, 1985.

Moltmann, E. and J. *Dieu, homme et femme.* Paris: Du Cerf, 1984.

Morin, E. *Jesus e as estruturas de seu tempo.* São Paulo: Paulinas, 1982.

Neusner, J. *Judaism in the Beginning of Christianity.* Philadelphia: Fortress, 1984.

Pascal, B. *Oeuvres Complètes.* Bibliothèque de la Pléiade. Paris: Gallimard, 1954.

Paul VI. *Marialis Cultus.*

Pellé-Douel, Y. *Étre femme.* Paris: Du Seuil, 1967.

Porciles Santiso, M. T. *A hora de Maria, A hora da mulher.* São Paulo: Paulinas, 1982.

Rahner, K. *Mary, Mother of the Lord: Theological Meditations.* New York: Herder and Herder, 1963.

Ricoeur, P. *The Conflict of Interpretations.* Evanston, Ill.: Northwestern University Press, 1974.

———. *Fallible Man.* New York: Fordham University Press, 1986.

———. *The Symbolism of Evil.* Boston: Beacon, 1969.

Ruether, R. R. *The Feminine Face of the Church.* Philadelphia: Westminster, 1977.

———. *New Woman, New Earth: Sexist Ideologies and Human Liberation.* New York: Seabury, 1975.

———. *Sexism and God-Talk.* Boston: Beacon, 1983.

Saint Yves, P. *As virgens mães e os nascimentos miraculosos.* Rio de Janeiro: Livraria Império Editora, n.d.

Schillebeeckx, E. *Mary: Mother of the Redemption.* 2nd ed. London and New York: Sheed and Ward, 1984.

Schüssler Fiorenza, E. *In Memory of Her: A Feminist Theological Reconstruction of Christian Origins.* New York: Crossroad, 1983.

Teresa, Saint. *The Collected Works of St. Teresa of Avila.* Washington: Institute of Carmelite Studies, 1976.

Ugarte, R. V. *Historia del culto a María en Iberoamérica.* Vols. 1 and 2. Madrid, 1956.

Valle, E., et al. *Evangelização e comportamento religioso popular.* Petrópolis: Vozes, 1978.

Various. *La sfida del femminismo alla teologia.* Brescia: Queriniana, 1969.

————. *Lo Spirito Santo e Maria Santissima*. Rome: Tipografia Poliglota Vaticana, 1973.

————. *Maria e la Chiesa oggi*. Rome: Ed. Marianum, 1985.

————. *Maria e lo Spirito Santo*. Rome: Ed. Marianum, 1984.

ARTICLES, REVIEWS, THESES

Benedetti, R. L. "A devoção a Nossa Senhora e as transformações sociais." *Vida Pastoral* (May-June, 1985).

Boff, L. "Constantes antropológicas e revelação." *REB* 32, fasc. 125 (March 1972), pp. 26-41.

Borresen, K. E. "L'anthropologie théologique d'Augustin et de Thomas d'Aquin." *Recherches de Science Religieuse* 69/3 (1981).

Bulletin de la Société Française d'études Mariales. 1968, 1969, 1970.

Carvalho Azevedo, M."A oração de Maria, intérprete da palavra." *Convergência* 189 (January 1986), pp. 56-64.

————. "A oração de Maria, testemunha da palavra." *Convergência* 190 (March 1986).

Cavalcanti, T. "Culto a María — tradição e renovação." *Grande Sinal* 40 (May 1986), pp. 267-278.

Concilium. No. 134: *Women in a Man's Church*. Edinburgh: T & T Clark; New York: Seabury, 1980.

Concilium. No. 168: *Mary in the Churches*. Edinburgh: T & T Clark; New York: Seabury, 1983.

Concilium. No. 173: *The Sexual Revolution*. 1984.

Couto Texeira, F. L. *A fé na vida: Um estudo teológico-pastoral sobre a experiência das CEBs no Brazil*. Doctoral thesis. Rome: Pontifical Gregorian University, 1985.

Nouvelle Revue Theologique 89, 1967.

Revista Eclesiastica Brasileira 46, fasc. 181 (March 1986): *Teologia feminista na América Latina*.

Ricoeur, P. "Nommer Dieu." *EthThR* 52 (1976), pp. 489-508.

Roy, A. "O mistério da mulher." *Convergência* 13, no. 135 (September 1980), pp. 415-421.

Tamez, E. "Agar, a mulher que complicou a história da salvação." *Por tras da palavra*, newsletter of CEBI. No. 27 (March-April, 1985).

Index